ENGLISH LITERATURE SKILLS

STUDYING THE NOVEL

by

Mary M. Firth   Andrew G. Ralston

Illustrations
by
Miranda E. Ralston

ISBN 0 340 810718

Hodder Gibson
2A Christie Street, Paisley, PA1 1NB

ACKNOWLEDGEMENTS

Extract from *The Third Man* by Graham Greene
Published by Vintage
Reprinted by permission of David Higham Associates Limited

Extract from *The Fallen Idol* by Graham Greene
Published by Vintage
Reprinted by permission of David Higham Associates Limited

Extract from *Lord of the Flies* by William Golding
Reprinted by permission of Faber and Faber

Extract from *The Great Gatsby* by F. Scott Fitzgerald
Published by Penguin
Reprinted by permission of David Higham Associates Limited

Extract from *Stars and Bars* by William Gibson
Reproduced by permission of Penguin Books Ltd

Silver from *The Sun's Net*
by George Mackay Brown
Reprinted by permission of John Murray (Publishers) Ltd

Photograph from *Pride and Prejudice* Video
Reprinted by permission of BBC Photograph Library

Photograph from *Great Expectations* Video
Reprinted by permission of BBC Photograph Library

Negative number E(Aus)1220 — Chateau Wood Ypres
Reprinted by kind permission of the Imperial War Museum

Negative number HU 41932 — Soldiers on Riot Control in Northern Ireland
Reprinted by kind permission of the Imperial War Museum

The publishers have wherever possible acknowledged the source of copyright material. They regret any inadvertent omission and will be pleased to make the necessary acknowledgement in future printings.

Orders: please contact Bookpoint Ltd, 130 Milton Park, Abingdon, Oxon OX14 4SB. Telephone: (44) 01235 827720. Fax. (44) 01235 400454. Lines are open from 9.00–6.00, Monday to Saturday, with a 24 hour message answering service. You can also order through our website www.hodderheadline.co.uk.

British Library Cataloguing in Publication Data
A catalogue record for this title is available from the British Library

ISBN 0 340 810 718

Published by Hodder Gibson, 2a Christie Street, Paisley PA1 1NB.
Tel: 0141 848 1609; Fax: 0141 889 6315; email: hoddergibson@hodder.co.uk
First Published 2003
Impression number   10 9 8 7 6 5 4 3 2 1
Year   2008 2007 2006 2005 2004 2003

Copyright © 2003 Mary M. Firth and Andrew G. Ralston

Cover photo from Getty Images.
Typeset by Fakenham Photosetting Limited.
Printed in Great Britain for Hodder Gibson, 2a Christie Street, Paisley, PA1 1NB, Scotland, UK by Bell & Bain.

SADI4 728

CONTENTS

INTRODUCTION

1.   The place of the novel in the current English syllabus

Examination regulations and course content are constantly evolving. Nevertheless, it is safe to say that any upper secondary school student pursuing a course in English Literature is likely at some stage to be required to write a detailed essay on, or review of, a novel.

The study of the modern novel is a key element of the course specifications of the examination systems in both England and Scotland:

- *Higher Level (Scotland)*: as one of the internal assessment tasks, pupils have the option of writing a review of a novel of their own choice.

- *Advanced Higher Level (Scotland)*: takes this task a stage further and requires a substantial dissertation on at least two linked texts.

- *AS Level (Module One–The Modern Novel)*: the AQA (Assessment and Qualifications Alliance) requires an essay to be written on one of the set texts.

- *Module 4 at Advanced (A2) Level*: allows pupils to write on one prose text and to compare this to another text of a different period, type or genre.

- *GCSE English Literature (Unit 2)*: involves the study of post-1914 prose.

2.   *English Literature Skills:* the aim

In the light of these syllabus requirements, this book aims to assist pupils to develop their skills in the literary analysis of prose fiction, and to suggest possible texts and areas of study.

3.   *English Literature Skills:* the structure

Part One: Approaching the Novel, takes four key elements that can be found in every work of fiction — theme, characterisation, setting and style — and explains, by means of extracts from both classic and modern novels and short stories, how these are handled by different writers. Questions for classroom discussion or written answers are provided.

Part Two: Analysing the Novel, provides advice on writing book reviews and comparative dissertations, again incorporating smaller practice exercises.

Part Three: Appreciating the Novel, gives plot summaries of sixteen modern novels in order to assist students in choosing the kind of book that is likely to appeal to them.

A deliberate attempt has been made to select a representative mix of works of fiction. A variety of well-known and established novels from the twentieth century are included, such as A*nimal Farm* or *The Old Man and the Sea,* as copies will generally be available in schools. Some of these books are currently GCSE set texts. At the same time, equal space is devoted to novels written in the last few years (some of them having won literary prizes or having been the basis of films) which those looking for guidance on a way into recent fiction can take as a starting point.

In each case, a short synopsis ('The Novel in a Nutshell') is given, together with an indication of the level of difficulty. This is followed by a more detailed outline and, under the title of 'Taking a closer look', some thoughts on thematic or stylistic issues that students might use as possible topics to write about.

Throughout the book, technical terms (symbolism, allegory and so on) are highlighted in **bold** type. At the end of the book there is a list of definitions of these terms which can be used for revision purposes.

MMF / AGR

PART ONE

APPROACHING THE NOVEL

UNDERSTANDING THE TASK

What *is* a book review?

You may be familiar with book reviews in newspapers and magazines. However, a book review which is part of an English course at school or college is different in several ways from such a review. In each case, the purpose is different.

The newspaper review

In the case of a newspaper or magazine review, the aim is to *inform* the reader about a newly published book and to present an opinion on it which will enable readers to decide whether or not they wish to read the book for themselves. The reviewer will not hesitate to give a negative opinion if he feels this is what the book deserves. In other words, it is *the book* which is on trial. As a professional journalist, whose job it is to sell newspapers, the reviewer will also be making an effort to attract and hold the reader's attention and will often write humorously or include personal anecdotes to make the piece entertaining in its own right.

The English course review

Within the context of an English course, however, your aims are different. Firstly, you will be encouraged to choose a book which is already accepted as an example of good writing and which is therefore considered likely to reward your in-depth study. Your task is to show your understanding and appreciation of the text. It is *your literary skills* which are being tested, not the book itself. A review for an English course should be written formally, and must not contain any material which does not refer directly to the text.

Does that mean I can't give my opinion? What if I don't like the book?

Yes, you may give your opinion. Expressing a genuine personal response is expected and an intelligent viewpoint will gain credit in the overall mark. However, it is always sensible to be positive: failure to appreciate a book of recognised merit may expose your own lack of understanding. If you do criticise the book, you must be precise and have good foundation for your criticism. You might find an inconclusive ending disappointing, for instance. More guidance on this aspect of the review is given in **Part Two** of this book.

What if I don't like the book at all?

It is unwise to choose a book that you dislike for your review. You are likely to produce a much better result if you write about a text which you have truly found enjoyable and absorbing. It is important to make your choice carefully by selecting a book with subject matter that appeals to you. **Part Three** of this book offers information on a range of texts which will help you to choose one that you can engage with. If you find after reading several chapters of a book that you are still not enjoying it, it is better to leave it and try something else.

Two basic approaches

There are two basic approaches to writing about a novel. You may either write a general review which looks at all aspects of the book, or you may select a particular aspect or element as the focus of your essay, such as the development of a character, the relationship between two characters or the importance of a feature such as the setting.

In **Part Two** of this book you will be given guidance in writing different types of review. Whichever type you do, you will be expected to show your understanding of the various elements of the novel.

There are four main elements to be considered in the study of a novel:

- Theme

- Characterisation

- Setting (both in place and time)

- Style

THEME

The term **theme** is used in a variety of ways. A rough definition might be 'what the book is about'. Sometimes theme is interpreted as a brief summary of the plot, for example, 'boy meets girl'.

A more useful definition of theme is 'a central concern of the text'. A novel with a 'boy meets girl' plot might deal with several additional issues, such as religion, social class or racism. Having identified the themes, it is important to consider how the author presents these. A work of literature does not generally teach the reader a lesson as such, but it does portray a 'slice of life' which provokes us to think, and we are invited to draw our own conclusions and make judgements on the basis of our observations.

Taking a closer look . . .

Charles Dickens' novel *Great Expectations* is an example of a text with a basic 'boy meets girl' storyline that incorporates several themes which lead us to think about various aspects of life.

The following brief outline will reveal some of the central concerns of the text:

> Ten-year-old Philip Pirrup, known as Pip, is an orphan who is being brought up by his sister and her kind-hearted husband, Joe Gargery, a blacksmith. Pip is asked to go to a grand house to play with a rich girl of his own age, Estella. The house is owned by Miss Havisham, an eccentric old woman who lives as a recluse after being jilted long ago on her wedding day. Estella, her adopted daughter, is very beautiful, and, young as he is, Pip falls in love with her, although he is aware she is proud and haughty. Estella despises Pip, calling him 'common', which makes him ashamed of himself and his up-bringing.
>
> A few years later, on the verge of adulthood, Pip is mysteriously given a large fortune. He turns his back on Joe whom he now sees as an embarrassment and goes to London, where he lives smartly and extravagantly. Pip hopes and believes Miss Havisham has given him the money so that he can marry Estella. However, his hopes are dashed. Estella coldly rejects him and marries someone wealthier. Pip discovers Miss Havisham had deliberately planned that Estella should break his heart as her revenge on the male sex for her own heartache. Miss Havisham suffers for her cruelty when she dies horribly in a fire after Estella has also abandoned her. Pip is mortified to learn that his benefactor is actually an ex-convict whom he had helped when he was a little boy.
>
> At the end of the book Pip feels ashamed of his snobbishness and ingratitude. He realises the value of the home and old friends he had previously rejected and he is reconciled with the faithful Joe. He finally meets up with Estella again. It has been revealed that the proud Estella is actually the daughter of the convict. She is also unhappy after a failed marriage with her abusive husband, and now that she too is kinder and humbler as a result of her suffering, she and Pip agree to be friends.

The following table shows some of the themes and the evidence from which we might deduce these. The first one is completed; try to fill in the others. If you have read the book, or seen a film or television adaptation, you may be able to answer in more detail and add other themes that you have noticed.

Theme	Evidence
The influence of money on character	After becoming wealthy, Pip despises those who really love him. He becomes snobbish and selfish.
Social Class	
Love	
Revenge	

For Practice

Read the outlines of the following novels and make tables similar to the one above. One or two main themes are given to start you off. This exercise could be done in pairs or groups.

1. *Lord of the Flies* by William Golding

During a war a few years into the future, a group of young boys is being evacuated when their plane crashes on a deserted tropical island. The pilot is killed and, since there are no adults, the boys must organise themselves in order to survive. At first the boys are delighted by their apparent freedom from authority. Two of the older boys, Ralph and Jack, compete to  be the leader of the group, and Ralph is elected. He is supported by a boy called Piggy who has sensible ideas but who is despised and bullied by the others, particularly Jack, as he is fat and wears glasses. At first the boys try to act in a civilised way, holding meetings at which a conch shell is held as a symbol of law and order, and voting on issues concerning their survival. But the boys enter into more savage behaviour, distracted by their fear of a 'beast' which they believe inhabits the island. Jack leads a group who succeed in killing a pig. Their pleasure in the act of killing eventually detracts from the more practical tasks such as building shelters and keeping a fire alight to attract passing ships which Ralph tries to encourage.

Jack's tribe breaks away from the main group, and Jack, who has always resented Ralph, becomes its leader. The tribe's behaviour becomes more irresponsible and outrageous. One night, in a bloodthirsty frenzy they kill Simon, a quiet thoughtful boy who has realised that the only 'beast' on the island is the evil within themselves. Ralph and Piggy also join in the 'dance' during which Simon is killed. More and more boys join Jack who seems to promise 'fun', but in fact quickly becomes a dictator, until Ralph and Piggy are left isolated. Finally, on a visit to Jack's hideout to recover Piggy's glasses (which have been stolen to make fire) Roger, one of Jack's tribe, kills Piggy by rolling a large boulder onto him. The whole tribe then tries to hunt Ralph down with fire and spears, but he is rescued at the moment of capture by a naval officer whose boat has been attracted to the island by the smoke from the fire.

Themes	Evidence
The good and evil within human nature	
Civilisation	
Power and Authority	
Survival	

2. *To Kill a Mocking-Bird* by Harper Lee

The book is set in the 1930s, a time of racial inequality. Lawyer Atticus Finch, a widower, lives in a small town in Mississippi with his two children, Jem and Scout. The children, encouraged by Dill, a young boy who visits every summer, become obsessed by a neighbour whom they have never seen called Arthur 'Boo' Radley. Arthur, a gentle and timid man, has lived as a recluse since getting into trouble as a teenager, but because the children have never seen him they imagine him as a monster with fangs dripping blood. They do not associate him with the little gifts they find in a hollow tree. Scout starts school, but Atticus has already taught her to read. He also teaches her to be tolerant of those who are disadvantaged and to imagine herself inside the skin of others so that she can understand their feelings.

Atticus is asked to defend a negro, Tom Robinson, who has been arrested on a charge of rape. The alleged victim is a poor white girl, Mayella Ewell. Both Atticus and his family suffer considerable verbal abuse as a result of Atticus's apparently pro-black stance. At one point, Atticus has to protect Tom from being lynched in the jailhouse by a group led by the father of one of Scout's school-friends, Mr Cunningham. The ugly scene is defused when Scout turns up and starts chatting to Mr Cunningham about his son.

At the trial, Atticus's skilful cross-examination of the witnesses makes it quite clear that Tom is innocent. Mayella had in fact been beaten by her father, Bob Ewell, because he had seen her making advances to Tom. Tom is nevertheless found guilty by the white jury, who would never consider finding in favour of a black person over a white one. However, Atticus is encouraged by the fact that the jury debated for several hours, instead of arriving at a verdict quickly. It turns out that Mr Cunningham, who was on the jury, argued in favour of acquitting Tom. Tom later dies when he is shot whilst trying to escape from prison. In revenge for being shown up in court by Atticus, Bob Ewell attacks Scout and Jem, but they are saved by Boo Radley, who emerges from his house and kills Ewell.

3. *The Great Gatsby* by F. Scott Fitzgerald

The narrator, Nick Carraway, moves to Long Island in New York, where he rents a modest house next door to an extravagant mansion owned by a mysterious young millionaire named Jay Gatsby. Gatsby, who was originally very poor, has apparently made his money in criminal activities such as the illegal liquor trade. He regularly throws huge and lavish parties to which all kinds of people are welcome, although the host himself always keeps a low profile.

Across the bay, in a more fashionable area inhabited by those with 'old' money, lives Nick's beautiful cousin, Daisy Buchanan and her wealthy husband, Tom. Tom is conducting an affair with a woman named Myrtle Wilson whose husband owns a garage. As a poor young officer during the second World War, Gatsby had been engaged to Daisy, but while he was away in Europe, she had retreated into her own social class and married Tom instead. Gatsby longs to be reunited with Daisy, and he has in fact bought the house in the hope that she may one day come to one of his parties, but Daisy moves in higher social circles and she never does. When Gatsby discovers Nick is Daisy's cousin, he arranges to meet Daisy at Nick's house. Following this, Gatsby sees Daisy regularly, and he secretly hopes she may be persuaded to leave Tom. However, one hot afternoon when they all go to New York city on an outing, feelings come to the surface.

They arrive at a hotel in two cars, with Tom driving Gatsby's large, distinctive yellow car. When Gatsby challenges Daisy to admit she still loves him, and not Tom, the best Daisy can say is that she 'loves him *too*'. Tom sees this as a victory as it is clear Daisy will never leave him, and he even invites Gatsby to take Daisy home. Daisy drives as she feels it will calm her nerves. However, as they pass the Wilson's garage, Myrtle, whose husband has discovered their affair, runs out to stop the car, believing it to be Tom driving. Daisy runs Myrtle down and she is killed. Following the accident, Gatsby takes the blame. When Myrtle's husband goes to the Buchanans looking for revenge, they tell him where to find Gatsby. Wilson shoots him and the Buchanans do not even go to his funeral. Apparently unconcerned about the deaths of both Myrtle and Gatsby, they go away to Europe together.

4. *The Third Man* by Graham Greene

The novel is set soon after the second World War. Rollo Martins, a writer of second rate Western novels, arrives in Vienna at the invitation of an old school friend, Harry Lime. He is shocked to discover that Harry has just been killed in a car accident and attends his funeral where he meets Colonel Calloway, a British police officer who is investigating black market dealings and associated criminal activities. When Calloway tells him Harry was mixed up in some very unsavoury deeds, including murder, Martins refuses to believe it, although during their school-days Harry had often got them both into trouble. He resolves to clear Harry's name and investigate Harry's death. He questions the caretaker at the flats where Harry lived and where the car accident took place, but soon after this, the caretaker is murdered. Martins meets up with Harry's girlfriend, Anna Schmidt, an actress, and tells her his suspicions. Leaving Anna's flat one night, Martins catches sight of a man's face illuminated by a window, and is shocked to recognise Harry himself. He sets off in pursuit, but Harry disappears. He later learns that Harry had escaped down a manhole into the sewers of the city.

Calloway questions Martins about the caretaker, and explains to him the charges against Harry. Harry had been part of a gang dealing in stolen penicillin. Their trade involved diluting the penicillin before selling it so that instead of curing patients it made their condition worse. In an outbreak of meningitis at a children's hospital, some children died, and others were brain damaged. Martins realises that the evidence against Harry is overwhelming and he feels disillusioned and let down. Martins tells Calloway that Harry is in fact alive, but he refuses to help trap him. Martins has fallen in love with Anna but his loyalty to his former friend does not waver and Anna says that she still loves Harry despite everything he has done.

Martins finally contacts Harry through a mutual acquaintance and they meet at the ferris wheel in the Prater pleasure gardens. Harry is charming but remains unrepentant. He readily confesses his crime, saying that he has done it purely for the money. The dead body at his 'funeral' was actually that of a former accomplice who had become a double agent. Martins finally loses all regard for his former friend, seeing him as shallow and evil. He is particularly enraged when Harry admits he traded information about Anna to the authorities in return for his own safety. Martins finally agrees to help the police to track Harry down. Harry again takes refuge in the sewers where he is hunted down and shot by Martins himself.

5. *Jane Eyre* by Charlotte Brontë

Jane Eyre, an orphan, is brought up by her wealthy aunt, Mrs Reed, who is cold and cruel and who allows her own three children to bully Jane. One day, after she has been taunted and hit by her cousin, John Reed, Jane retaliates. Mrs Reed sends her to Lowood, a girls' boarding school where conditions are grim. However, Jane makes a friend, Helen Burns, who inspires her with her calmness and patience. Helen is victimised by one of the teachers and later dies in an epidemic which breaks out at the school. After this, conditions improve, and Jane stays on and becomes a teacher.

Jane then goes to work at a great house called Thornfield Hall as a governess to a little girl whose guardian is the wealthy but severe Mr Rochester. Jane saves his life when a fire breaks out in his room. Although Jane is poor, plain and friendless, Mr Rochester values her honesty and sincerity above the glamour of the society beauty Blanche Ingram, who has ambitions to marry him and become mistress of Thornfield. Jane is overjoyed and amazed to receive a proposal of marriage from Rochester, but at their wedding a mysterious stranger appears and stops the proceedings by revealing that Rochester is already married. His wife is a madwoman who is locked up in the attic, and had escaped to start the fire.

Jane leaves at once, taking no money or possessions. She is taken in by a clergyman called St John Rivers and his sisters. After some time, St John proposes marriage to Jane, but she refuses, remaining loyal in her heart to Rochester. One night she dreams she hears him calling, and is certain something is wrong. She sets out for Thornfield to discover that there has been another fire in which Rochester's wife has died. Rochester has survived but has been blinded. Jane and he are finally married, and both are restored to happiness.

CHARACTERISATION

The term 'characterisation' means the creation and presentation of characters. A writer will aim to provoke a particular response from the reader through the actions and experiences of his characters.

What's in a Name?

One of the simplest ways in which an author will try to establish a character is by the choice of name.

In the past, authors sometimes chose names which made clear some aspect of the character's role or personality and this practice is still sometimes followed today. For example, William Thackeray chose the name Becky *Sharp* for the anti-heroine of his novel, *Vanity Fair*. Becky Sharp is a ruthless and clever social climber, who is sharp by nature as well as by name. In *The Prime of Miss Jean Brodie*, a novel in which a teacher called Jean Brodie is forced to resign when a favourite pupil gives the headmistress information about her, the girl who betrays her is called Sandy *Stranger*. The character's name is a clue to the fact that Miss Brodie does not know Sandy as well as she thinks she does.

More recently, there have been similar examples of descriptive names. The crime writer Ian Rankin has chosen the name John *Rebus* for his detective. A 'rebus' is a puzzle, which makes it a suitable name for a clever man who solves crimes. Occasionally there may be a twist in the choice of a character's name. In Janice Galloway's novel *The Trick is To Keep Breathing*, which is about a woman undergoing a nervous breakdown, the character is ironically named *Joy*.

For Practice

1. Look at the names of the characters in Thomas Hardy's *The Woodlanders* on page 26. Discuss how appropriate the names seem to be for the characters.

2. In Charlotte Brontë's *Jane Eyre*, (summarised on pages 12–13), two of the teachers at Lowood, Jane's boarding school, are called Miss Temple and Miss Scatcherd. One is strict and cruel; the other kind and understanding. Which name do you think suits each teacher and why?

3. What do you think the names of the following characters might suggest about them? The novel in which they appear is in brackets.

   (a) Mr Knightley (*Emma* by Jane Austen)

   (b) Gabriel Oak (*Far From the Madding Crowd* by Thomas Hardy)

   (c) Damon Wildeve (*The Return of the Native* by Thomas Hardy)

   (d) Mr Smallweed (*Bleak House* by Charles Dickens)

   (e) Mrs Proudie (*Barchester Towers* by Anthony Trollope)

   (f) Frank Cauldhame (*The Wasp Factory* by Iain Banks)

   (g) Holly Golightly (*Breakfast at Tiffany's* by Truman Capote)

   (h) Scout Finch (*To Kill a Mocking-Bird* by Harper Lee – Think of the significance of 'scout')

   (i) Edith Hope (*Hotel du Lac* by Anita Brookner – Edith is a romantic novelist whose own love life is unsatisfactory)

   (j) Mr Wickham (*Pride and Prejudice* by Jane Austen – Wickham is the villain of the novel)

Presenting a Personality

If a writer wishes us to approve of an attitude or type of behaviour, or to sympathise with the situation of a character, he will usually give the character appealing and admirable traits. This can be seen in the novel *To Kill a Mocking-Bird* (outlined on page 9), which explores and condemns racial prejudice. The character of Atticus, the lawyer who takes a courageous stand in defending a negro, is presented as a model human being : infinitely patient, kind and loving to his children; respectful to his black housekeeper; tolerant and forgiving of others. While many readers find the character too good to be true, the author, Harper Lee, aims to make her own views on race more acceptable to the reader by presenting them through a character who has no apparent faults.

In analysing characterisation for a book review, you should consider two main aspects:

- the portrayal and development of individual characters
- the way relationships between characters are portrayed and developed.

For Practice (1)

Look at the following descriptions of characters, and consider the effect the author is trying to create. Each description is placed in context to help you.

(a) Extract from *The Third Man* by Graham Greene.

> *Context:* *The narrator is a policeman, Colonel Calloway, who is conducting a criminal investigation into a man called Harry Lime who is the mastermind of a racket involving stolen penicillin (see the outline on pages 11–12). Calloway is trying to persuade one of Lime's oldest friends that he should help turn him in to the police.*

Don't picture Harry Lime as a smooth scoundrel. He wasn't that. The picture I have of him on my file is an excellent one: he is caught by a street photographer with his stocky legs apart, big shoulders a little hunched, a belly that has known too much good food for too long, on his face a look of cheerful rascality, a geniality, a recognition that his happiness will make the world's day.

Questions

1. *Which expressions present Lime as an attractive character whom his friend will find difficult to betray?*

2. *What clues are there to Lime's basic selfishness?*

3. *Are there any details which suggest he will be a tough opponent?*

(b) Extract from *The Aspern Papers* by Henry James.

Context : The narrator is a great admirer of a famous poet who died long ago, but whose mistress, Juliana, is still alive and living in Venice. This woman had been a great beauty in her youth and inspired wonderful love poetry. The writer hopes to obtain some of the poet's personal papers from her, and is thrilled and intrigued at the prospect of a meeting, as she seems like a link with the past.

She had over her eyes a horrible green shade which served for her almost as a mask. I believed for the instant that she had put it on expressly, so that from underneath it she might take me all in without my getting at herself. At the same time it created a presumption of some ghastly death's-head lurking behind it. The divine Juliana as a grinning skull – the vision hung there until it passed. Then it came to me that she was tremendously old — so old that death might take her at any moment. She was very small and shrunken, bent forward with her hands in her lap. She was dressed in black and her head was wrapped in a piece of old black lace which showed no hair.

Questions

1. *Which details particularly contrast with the narrator's former image of Juliana as a beautiful woman capable of inspiring great passion?*

2. *Which details suggest Juliana will be quite evil?*

(c)   Extract from *Jane Eyre* by Charlotte Brontë.

      Context: *The narrator, Jane, is an orphan and a poor relation, being brought up by her aunt, Mrs Reed, who has a son, John.*

John Reed was a schoolboy of fourteen years old — four years older than I, for I was but ten; large and stout for his age, with a dingy and unwholesome skin; heavy limbs and large extremities. He gorged himself habitually at table, which made him bilious, and gave him a dim and bleared eye and flabby cheeks. He ought now to have been at school, but his mamma had taken him home for a month or two, "on account of his delicate health." Mr Miles, the master, affirmed that he would do very well if he had fewer cakes and sweetmeats sent him from home; but the mother's heart turned from an opinion so harsh, and inclined rather to the idea that his sallowness was owing to over-application and, perhaps, to pining after home. John had not much affection for his mother and sister, and an antipathy to me. He bullied and punished me, not two or three times in the week, nor once or twice in the day, but continually; every nerve I had feared him, and every morsel of flesh on my bones shrank when he came near. The servants did not like to offend their young master by taking my part against him, and Mrs Reed was blind and deaf on the subject. She never saw him strike or heard him abuse me, though he did both now and then in her very presence; more frequently, however, behind her back.

Questions

1. *Explain which expressions make the character of John Reed physically repulsive to you.*

2. *Which techniques does the author use to ensure that the reader identifies entirely with Jane rather than John?*

(d) Extract from *The Fallen Idol* by Graham Greene.

Context: *Philip is a young boy whose wealthy parents are often abroad. They leave him in the care of the butler and his wife, Mr and Mrs Baines. Mr Baines is kind and friendly to Philip, while his wife is sharp and severe. Baines is having an affair with a younger woman and he has invited her to the house while his wife is away. However, because of information Philip has innocently let slip, Mrs Baines has become suspicious and returns hoping to trap her husband and his lover. She creeps into Philip's room after he has fallen asleep to question him.*

He opened his eyes and saw Mrs Baines was there, her grey untidy hair in threads over his face, her black hat askew. A loose hairpin fell on the pillow and one musty thread brushed his mouth. 'Where are they?' she whispered. 'Where are they?'

Philip watched her in terror. With her untidy grey hair and her black dress buttoned to her throat, her gloves of black cotton, she was so like the witches of his dreams that he didn't dare to speak. There was a stale smell in her breath.

'She's here,' Mrs Baines said, 'you can't deny she's here.' Her face was simultaneously marked with cruelty and misery; she wanted to 'do things' to people, but she suffered all the time. It would have done her good to scream, but she daren't do that: it would warn them.

Questions

1.   *What details do you find particularly effective in showing Mrs Baines as an object of terror to Philip?*

2.   *How far does the author lead the reader to feel sympathy for Mrs Baines?*

(e)   Extract from *Far From the Madding Crowd* by Thomas Hardy.

> *Context :   Gabriel Oak, the hero of the novel which is set in the nineteenth century, catches sight for the first time of the girl with whom he will fall in love. She is riding on top of a cart piled with her possessions as she is moving house. The cart has stopped briefly.*

The wagon was laden with household goods and window plants, and on the apex of the whole sat a woman, young and attractive. The girl waited for some time idly in her place. Then she looked attentively downwards at an oblong package tied in paper. At length she drew the article into her lap and untied the paper covering; a small swing looking-glass was disclosed, in which she proceeded to survey herself attentively. She parted her lips and smiled.

It was a fine morning, and the sun lighted up to a scarlet glow the crimson jacket she wore and painted a soft lustre upon her bright face and dark hair. What possessed her to indulge in such a performance nobody knows; it ended certainly in a real smile. There was no necessity whatever for her looking in the glass. She did not adjust her hat, or pat her hair, or press a dimple into shape. She simply observed herself as a fair product of Nature, her thoughts seeming to glide into far-off though likely dramas in which men would play a part — vistas of probable triumphs.

Question

Looking at all the evidence in the extract, assess how appealing the character of the girl is to the reader.

For Practice (2)

Look at the following extracts from *Lord of the Flies* by William Golding. They present the developing relationship between the characters of Ralph (the fair boy) and Piggy (the fat boy), two of the children stranded without any adults on an island after a plane crash. (Ralph is later elected chief by the group.) Your task is to explain how the relationship between the boys changes from one stage in the book to the next.

(a)   The fair boy began to pick his way as casually as possible towards the water. He tried to be offhand and not too obviously uninterested, but the fat boy hurried after him.

"Aren't there any grown-ups at all?"

"I don't think so."

The fair boy said this solemnly; but then the delight of a realised ambition overcame him. In the middle of the scar he stood on his head and grinned at the reversed fat boy.

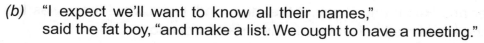

"No grown-ups!"

(b)   "I expect we'll want to know all their names," said the fat boy, "and make a list. We ought to have a meeting."

Ralph did not take the hint so the fat boy was forced to continue.

"I don't care what they call me," he said confidentially, "so long as they don't call me what they used to call me at school."

Ralph was faintly interested.

"What was that?"

The fat boy glanced over his shoulder, then leaned towards Ralph.

He whispered.

"They used to call me 'Piggy'."

Ralph shrieked with laughter.

(c)   Ralph turned and smiled involuntarily. Piggy was a bore; …but there was always a little pleasure to be got out of pulling his leg, even if one did it by accident. Piggy saw the smile and misinterpreted it as friendliness.

(d)   Ralph moved impatiently. The trouble was, if you were a chief you had to think, you had to be wise.
       Only, decided Ralph as he faced the chief's seat, I can't think. Not like Piggy. Once more that evening Ralph had to adjust his values. Piggy could think.

(e)   Ralph rolled over.
       "Piggy. What are we going to do?"
       "Just have to get on without 'em."
       "But – the fire."
       He frowned at the black and white mess in which lay the unburnt ends of branches. He tried to formulate.
       "I'm scared."

(f)   The four biguns crept into the shelter and burrowed under the leaves. The twins lay together and Ralph and Piggy at the other end. For a while there was the continual creak and rustle of leaves as they tried for comfort.
       "Piggy."
       "Yeah?"
       "All right?"
       "S'pose so."

Complete the box on the following page to show how the relationship between the boys progresses.

(a) The very simple descriptions: 'the fair boy'; 'the fat boy'; suggest contrasting schoolboy stereotypes: Ralph will be attractive and popular, and Piggy a figure of fun. Ralph is athletic, doing gymnastics, while Piggy just watches him. Piggy is obviously the follower: 'hurried after him'. Ralph does not want Piggy's company and gives him no encouragement, speaking in an 'offhand' way, but tries to be tactful 'not too obviously uninterested.' Ralph is happy and good-humoured and is willing to include Piggy in his delight at the freedom from authority: 'grinned'.

(b)

(c)

(d)

(e) The relationship is now much closer and more even, shown by the equal length of their speeches. The shortness of the speeches suggests they have a close understanding and sympathy for one another. Ralph starts the conversation, revealing he is no longer detached and uninterested and shows concern for Piggy by asking how he is feeling.

SETTING

Readers sometimes wonder why writers spend so much time on description, particularly of the background settings.

WHY DOESN'T HE JUST GET ON WITH TELLING THE STORY?

History and Geography

Description isn't necessarily there for its own sake, or just to fill up paper. If a book is set in a particular period of history, such as the Second World War (1939–45) or the French Revolution (1789), the author may devote some space to describing typical features of life at the time to make the story more realistic.

The setting of a book can be geographical as well as historical. Locating events in real places can be an important element of stories which involve a journey, an expedition or a chase. For example, in John Buchan's novel *The Thirty-Nine Steps* the hero, Richard Hannay, is chased across the countryside of the Scottish Borders by his enemies. Buchan takes the real landscape of the Moffat area and adds his own fictional landmarks to it. Novels of this kind often contain a map to allow the reader to trace the journey.

Similarly, the modern crime writer Ian Rankin gives his novels a gritty realism by locating events in various streets and districts of the city of Edinburgh. He frequently draws a contrast between wealthy fashionable areas and deprived, rundown ones.

Sherlock Holmes Investigates

An earlier crime writer was Sir Arthur Conan Doyle, creator of the famous detective Sherlock Holmes. *The Valley of Fear* concerns Holmes' investigation of a grim murder in an English country house. Early in the story the following passage describes the setting of the crime:

About half a mile from the town, standing in an old park famous for its huge beech trees, is the ancient Manor House of Birlstone. Part of this venerable building dates back to the time of the first Crusade, when Hugo de Capus built a fort in the centre of the estate, which had been granted to him by the Red King. This was destroyed by fire in 1543, and some of its smoke-blackened corner-stones were used when, in Jacobean times, a brick country house rose upon the ruins of the feudal castle. The Manor House, with its many gables and its small, diamond-paned windows, was still much as the builder had left it in the early seventeenth century. Of the double moats which had guarded its more warlike predecessor the outer had been allowed to dry up, and served the humble function of a kitchen garden. The inner one was still there, and lay, forty feet in breadth, though now only a few feet in depth, round the whole house. The ground floor windows were within a foot of the surface of the water. The only approach to the house was over a drawbridge which was not only capable of being raised, but actually was raised every evening and lowered every morning. By thus renewing the custom of the old feudal days the Manor House was converted into an island during the night.

Questions

This might appear to be an unimportant section of the book, and the reader might wish to hurry on to see when a crime was going to take place.

1. Why do you think the author includes the historical details?

2. Why does he give such precise details about the house and its surroundings?

3. Bearing in mind that this passage comes from a crime novel, which features mentioned might have a direct bearing on the story to be told?

Taking a closer look . . .

Most books have some kind of background setting in time or place. But there are others where the setting plays a much larger role. *The Woodlanders* by Thomas Hardy is a good example of this kind of book. Written in 1887, it tells a tragic love story involving six connected characters:

George Melbury

A comfortably-off timber merchant who has used his wealth to give his daughter Grace an expensive education

Grace Melbury

Beautiful and accomplished, she has nevertheless not completely shaken off her country upbringing

Giles Winterbourne

A poor but honest timber worker who still loves Grace, his childhood sweetheart

Dr Fitzpiers

The superficially more attractive but unfaithful local doctor whom Grace marries

Marty South

A poor girl who loves Giles faithfully but is too shy to tell him

Mrs Charmond

A wealthy local landowner and 'femme fatale' with whom Fitzpiers has an affair

Practically all the action takes place in a small village called Little Hintock and in the woodlands surrounding it. Little Hintock is an imaginary place in the area of the south of England that Hardy called Wessex — largely based on the county of Dorset.

The Woodlanders shows some of the ways that a writer can use setting to develop his characters and themes.

- Even the title of the book points to the fact that the lives of the characters are bound up with their setting: what these people have in common is that they belong to the woodland and, in one way or another, derive their living from it.

- A good example is Marty South's father, who is very ill and who lives under the delusion that a certain tree outside his window, which was exactly the same age as him, is going to fall on him and kill him.

  Dr Fitzpiers, being an outsider and not understanding woodland ways, thinks the remedy is to have the tree cut down, but when this is done Old South dies of shock.

- Giles and Marty live particularly close to nature. Giles has 'a marvellous power of making trees grow.' At the end of the novel, when Giles is dead, Marty says:

  'Whenever I plant the young larches I'll think that none can plant as you planted.'

  The ongoing work of planting, tending and pruning is her way of keeping faith with Giles.

For practice (1)

Read the following passage which describes the character of Giles after he has been working at cider-making and the effect this has on Grace Melbury, the woman he has always loved, who is now trapped in an unhappy marriage to the unfaithful Dr Fitzpiers.

He looked and smelt like Autumn's very brother, his face being sunburnt to wheat-colour, his eyes blue as cornflowers, his sleeves and leggings dyed with fruit-stains, his hands clammy with the sweet juice of apples, his hat sprinkled with pips, and everywhere about him that atmosphere of cider which at its first return each season has such an indescribable fascination for those who have been born and bred among the orchards.

Her heart rose from its late sadness like a released bough; her senses revelled in the sudden lapse back to Nature unadorned. The consciousness of having to be genteel because of her husband's profession, the veneer of artificiality which she had acquired at the fashionable schools, were thrown off, and she became the crude country girl of her latent early instincts.

Nature was bountiful, she thought. No sooner had she been cast aside by Edred Fitzpiers than another being, impersonating chivalrous and undiluted manliness, had arisen out of the earth ready to her hand.

Questions

The writer has created numerous links between characters, themes and the setting of the novel. The following questions will assist you in analysing how Thomas Hardy has achieved this.

1. In the first paragraph, there is one basic comparison which is then developed via a number of different detailed variations.

    (a) What is the main comparison in the first line?
    (b) How is this developed in the following five lines?
    (c) Which figures of speech are used in this description of Giles?
    (d) Choose any one of these and explain why it is effective — i.e., what light does it shed on the character or appearance of Giles?

2. In the second paragraph Hardy describes the effect of seeing Giles on Grace.

   (a) How does the opening simile convey her feelings?

   (b) How does this comparison relate to the wider setting of the book?

   (c) 'Her senses revelled in the sudden lapse back to Nature unadorned'. What do you take this to mean?

   (d) What is Hardy implying through his use of words like 'having to be', 'veneer' and 'artificiality'? A 'veneer' is a thin layer of a better quality outer material fixed to the surface of an inferior material, such as a real wood veneer finish. Consider why this word is appropriate here.

   (e) What is implied by the use of words like 'thrown off', 'crude', 'latent' and 'instincts'?

   (f) What do your answers to (d) and (e) above tell you about one of the main themes of the novel?

For practice (2)

In the following passage, a description of nature is used for the purpose of creating a different kind of mood. Grace has been deserted by her unfaithful husband; her childhood love, Giles, has lost his home and is dying. While Grace wonders what has happened to Giles, the following description of the woods is given:

In front lay the brown leaves of last year, and upon them some yellowish green ones of this season that had been prematurely blown down by the gale. Above stretched an old beech, with vast arm-pits, and great pocket-holes in its sides where branches had been removed in past times ... Dead boughs were scattered about and beyond them were perishing woodbine stems resembling old ropes.

Next were more trees close together, wrestling for existence, their branches disfigured with wounds resulting from their mutual rubbings and blows. It was the struggle between these neighbours that she had heard in the night. Beneath them were the rotting stumps of those of the group that had been vanquished long ago, rising from their mossy setting like black teeth from green gums.

The strain upon Grace's mind in various ways was so great on this the most desolate day she had passed there that she felt it would be well-nigh impossible to spend another in such circumstances.

Clearly, Grace is depressed and anxious. Make a list of all the words, phrases and figures of speech used to describe the trees which also reflect Grace's feelings.

STYLE:

(1) NARRATIVE POINT OF VIEW

The first aspect of the style of writing in any novel is the narrative point of view. In other words, through whose eyes is the story being told?

A novelist can basically take one of two approaches:

- he can write from his own point of view as the creator of all the characters in the book

- he can pretend to be one of the characters himself

The technical name for the first approach is an **omniscient narrator**. 'Omniscient' comes from Latin roots means 'all knowing'.

In real life, we can never be sure what another person is really thinking. Someone might put on a convincing show of friendship but may really be full of hatred or jealousy. Again, in real life we can often misinterpret people's behaviour or intentions because we cannot fully know what is going on in their minds. A girl treats a boy in a friendly way and he thinks she is particularly fond of him; she, however, just happens to have an outgoing personality and treats everyone she meets in the same manner.

An omniscient narrator has the advantage that he can see into all his characters' minds. He can not only write about how people behave outwardly to each other, but can also analyse their inner thoughts that they do not share with anyone else.

Some novelists, however, deliberately limit their viewpoint to that of one of their characters. They decide to tell the story through that character's eyes, with all the limitations that may impose. Such a story is told through a **persona** — that is, the author pretends to be one of his characters. This approach usually makes use of the first person ('I').

Within these two basic approaches, of course, there are many other narrative devices. Some novels vary the narrative approach by using the letter or diary form.

Taking a closer look . . .

This passage comes from the opening page of Graham Greene's novel *The Third Man*. (See pages 11–12 for a summary of what this book is about). Here is the opening section of the novel, and it employs a rather unusual story-telling approach:

One never knows when the blow may fall. When I saw Rollo Martins first I made this note on him for my security police files: 'In normal circumstances a cheerful fool. Drinks too much and may cause a little trouble. Whenever a woman passes raises his eyes and makes some comment, but I get the impression that really he'd rather not be bothered. Has never really grown up and perhaps that accounts for the way he worshipped Lime.' I wrote there that phrase 'in normal circumstances' because I met him first at Harry Lime's funeral. It was February, and the gravediggers had been forced to use electric drills to open the frozen ground in Vienna's Central Cemetery. It was as if even nature were doing its best to reject Lime, but we got him in at last and laid the earth back on him like bricks. He was vaulted in, and Rollo Martins walked quickly away as though his long gangly legs wanted to break into a run, and the tears of a boy ran down his thirty-five-year-old face. Rollo Martins believed in friendship, and that was why what happened later was a worse shock to him than it would have been to you or me. If only he had come to tell me then, what a lot of trouble would have been saved.

- Graham Greene is beginning with the end of the story here: we are told that Harry Lime, the key figure in the plot, is dead.

- The story is told through the eyes of one of the characters, Calloway the policeman. Greene is therefore using a **persona**.

- Calloway's comments in this opening paragraph show that he is able to look back on events with the benefit of hindsight — knowing how things ended, he is able to recount the sequence of events with more knowledge than was available at the time they were actually taking place. (Pick out the sentences or phrases which make this clear.) This method of storytelling is known as 'retrospective narration'. Which events referred to in the above extract do you think will be explained more fully later on in the story?

For Practice

Discuss the following extracts from fiction with a partner or in groups. For each of the extracts, you might consider points such as these:

- Who is telling the story?
- Is there an omniscient narrator or a persona?
- At what point in the sequence of events is the story being told?
- Are things happening now or is there retrospective narration?
- Is the narrator simply narrating, or is he / she trying to influence the opinion of the reader?
- Are you aware of any particular tone — humour, sarcasm, etc.? If so, which words / phrases help to establish this tone?
- Are any clues given about events that are to unfold later in the story?
- What insights are there into the characters or themes of the novel?

Don't just go through this list mechanically! What other features of the story-teller's approach do **YOU** notice?

1.   From *Breakfast at Tiffany's* by Truman Capote (1958)

I am always drawn back to places where I have lived, the houses and their neighbourhoods. For instance, there is a brownstone in the East Seventies where, during the early years of the war, I had my first New York apartment. It was one room crowded with attic furniture, a sofa and fat chairs upholstered in that itchy, particular red velvet that one associates with hot days on a train. The walls were stucco*, and a colour rather like tobacco-spit. Everywhere, in the bathroom too, there were prints of Roman ruins freckled brown with age. The single window looked out on a fire escape. Even so, my spirits heightened whenever I felt in my pocket the key to this apartment; with all its gloom, it still was a place of my own, the first, and my books were there, and jars of pencils to sharpen, everything I needed, so I felt, to become the writer I wanted to be.

It never occurred to me in those days to write about Holly Golightly, and probably it would not now except for a conversation I had with Joe Bell that set the whole memory of her in motion again.

* stucco: plaster or cement used for coating walls

2.   From *The Great Gatsby* by F. Scott Fitzgerald (1926)

In my younger and more vulnerable years my father gave me some advice that I've been turning over in my mind ever since.

'Whenever you feel like criticising anyone,' he told me, 'just remember that all the people in this world haven't had the advantages that you've had.'

He didn't say any more, but we've always been unusually communicative in a reserved way, and I understand that he meant a great deal more than that. In consequence, I'm inclined to reserve all judgments, a habit that has opened up many curious natures to me, and also made me the victim of not a few veteran bores. The abnormal mind is quick to detect and attach itself to this quality when it appears in a normal person, and so it came about that in college I was unjustly accused of being a politician, because I was privy to the secret griefs of wild, unknown men. Most of the confidences were unsought — frequently I have feigned sleep, preoccupation, or a hostile levity* when I realised by some unmistakable sign that an intimate revelation was quivering on the horizon.

* levity: lack of seriousness

3.   From *Stars and Bars* by William Boyd (1984)

Look at Henderson Dores walking up Park Avenue in New York City. 'I'm late,' he is thinking; and he is, late for work. He is carrying his sabres in a thin bag over his right shoulder and trying to appear calm and at ease, but that permanently worried expression on his square open face gives him away rather. The crowds of Americans — neat, well dressed — stride past him purposefully, unheeding, confident.

Henderson walks on. He is nearly forty years old — birthday coming up fast — and just under six feet tall. His frame is sturdy and his face is kind and agreeably attractive. To his constant surprise, people are inclined to like him on first acquaintance. He is polite, quite smartly dressed and, apart from that slight frown buckling his forehead he seems as composed and as unconcerned as, well, as you or me. But Henderson has a complaint, a grudge, a grumble of a deep and insidious kind. He doesn't like himself any more: isn't happy with the personality he's been provided with, thank you very much. Something about him isn't up to scratch, won't do. He'll keep the flesh, but he'd like to do a deal on the spirit, if nobody minds. He wants to change — he wants to be different from what he is. And that, really, is why he is here.

4.   From *The Tell-Tale Heart* by Edgar Allan Poe

True! — nervous — very, very, dreadfully nervous I had been and am; but why will you say that I am mad? The disease had sharpened my senses — not destroyed — not dulled them. Above all was the sense of hearing acute. I heard all things in the heaven and in the earth. I heard many things in hell. How, then, am I mad? Hearken! and observe how healthily — how calmly I can tell you the whole story.

It is impossible to say how first the idea entered my brain: but once conceived, it haunted me day and night. Object there was none. Passion there was none. I loved the old man. He had never wronged me. He had never given me insult. For his gold I had no desire. I think it was his eye! Yes, it was this! One of his eyes resembled that of a vulture — a pale blue eye, with a film over it. Whenever it fell upon me, my blood ran cold; and so by degrees — very gradually — I made up my mind to take the life of the old man, and thus rid myself of the eye forever.

5.   From *Wuthering Heights* by Emily Brontë (1847)

I have just returned from a visit to my landlord — the solitary neighbour that I shall be troubled with. This is certainly a beautiful country! In all England, I do not believe that I could have fixed on a situation so completely removed from the stir of society. A perfect misanthropist's* heaven; and Mr. Heathcliff and I are such a suitable pair to divide the desolation between us. A capital fellow! He little imagined how my heart warmed towards him when I beheld his black eyes withdraw suspiciously under their brows, as I rode up, and when his fingers sheltered themselves, with a jealous resolution, still further in his waistcoat, as I announced my name.

'Mr. Heathcliff!' I said.

A nod was the answer.

'Mr. Lockwood, your new tenant, sir. I do myself the honour of calling as soon as possible after my arrival, to express the hope that I have not inconvenienced you by my perseverance in soliciting the occupation of Thrushcross Grange: I heard yesterday you had had some thoughts —'

'Thrushcross Grange is my own, sir,' he interrupted wincing. 'I should not allow any one to inconvenience me, if I could hinder it — walk in!'

The 'walk in' was uttered with closed teeth and expressed the sentiment 'go to the deuce'; and I think that circumstance determined me to accept the invitation: I felt interested in a man who seemed more exaggeratedly reserved than myself.

* misanthropist: someone who hates the company of other human beings.

(2) SYMBOLISM

Symbolism is a technique by which an author presents an image which conveys a particular meaning or message to the reader. Once you have learned to recognise this technique it can be interesting and rewarding to explore the use of symbols in your chosen text.

Taking a closer look . . .

The novel *To Kill a Mocking-Bird* by Harper Lee deals with racism in the Southern States of America. (See the outline on page 9 if you have never read it.)

At the end of the first section there is an episode when Jem, the older of lawyer Atticus Finch's two children, knocks the heads off a neighbour's camellia flowers after she has abused Atticus for his pro-negro stance. Jem is made to apologise and to visit the old lady to atone for this. Shortly before she dies, the woman sends Jem a box containing a perfect white camellia flower. Part one of the book ends with Jem touching the beautiful flower thoughtfully. The fact that this episode is prominently placed at the end of the section suggests it has a special significance.

The camellia flower can be seen as a symbol of several things:

- It is a symbol of peace and reconciliation between Jem and the old woman.

- More generally, it is a symbol of hope, because it not only marks their reconciliation, but also is a reminder of the beauty of life.

- Being white and perfect it can symbolise the children's innocence, which is soon to be tarnished by their exposure to the evils of racism and the rape case.

- As the flower is delicate and will not last, it suggests vulnerability and mortality. This is significant both with reference to Tom Robinson, the negro who dies, and to the sensitive and misjudged character of Arthur Radley.

For Practice (1)

Read again the outline of the novel *To Kill a Mocking-Bird* by Harper Lee on page 9. The 'mocking-bird' of the title is taken from an apparently minor incident in the book. The children are given air-guns for Christmas, and told that they may shoot blue-jays, which are pests, but that they should never kill a mocking-bird which does no harm and brings nothing but joy to the world by its singing. At the end of the book, when Arthur Radley emerges from hiding to save the children, Scout agrees they should not tell anyone about his heroic action as publicity would be hurtful and damaging to such a shy man.

Question
In what way might the mocking-bird symbolise this? What other episode in the plot might the same symbol refer to?

For Practice (2)

Read again the outline of *Lord of the Flies* by William Golding (pages 7–8). There are many striking symbols in this novel. For example, there is the island itself. This can be seen as a symbol of the world at large and the children who inhabit it as the adult community. The island and the children are like a miniaturised and simplified version of the adult world.

Look at the following extracts and consider what might be symbolised in each:

(a) The children who came along the beach, singly or in twos, leapt into visibility when they crossed the line from heat-haze to nearer sand. Here the eye was first attracted to a black, bat-like creature that danced on the sand, and only later perceived the body above it. The bat was the child's shadow….

Question
What do you think the black shadow might symbolise? Why do you think the writer compares it to a bat?

(b) *The children find a conch shell which is rare and valuable. At first, during their meetings, everyone listens to whoever is holding the conch.*

In colour the shell was deep cream, touched here and there with fading pink. Between the point worn away into a little hole, and the pink lips of the mouth, lay eighteen inches of shell with a slight spiral twist and covered with a delicate embossed pattern.

Question

At this point, what is the conch a symbol of? What impression is created by the detailed description of the beauty and fragility of the shell?

(c) *Later, democracy and free speech are abandoned. Jack becomes a dictator. The conch is finally broken.*

By him [Ralph] stood Piggy still holding out the talisman, the fragile, shining beauty of the shell . . . The rock struck Piggy a glancing blow from chin to knee; the conch exploded into a thousand white fragments and ceased to exist.

Question

What might the breaking of the conch symbolise? Why should the author again draw attention to its beauty at this point?

(d) *A very common type of symbolism is to do with the weather. The weather is seen to reflect happenings on earth. For example, sunny weather will represent happiness; stormy weather will reflect some sort of upheaval.*

Over the island the build-up of clouds continued. A steady current of heated air rose all day from the mountain and was thrust to ten thousand feet; revolving masses of gas piled up the static until the air was ready to explode. By early evening the sun had gone and a brassy glare had taken the place of clear daylight.

Question

Which episode mentioned in the outline of the plot do you feel is most likely to follow this description?

The following story, *Silver,* by George Mackay Brown, is full of symbolism. Read it, and then answer the questions which follow.

SILVER

'You'll never get her,' said the skipper of the Kestrel. 'She's meant for some rich farmer on the hill.' He shook his head.

The three other fishermen of the Kestrel shook their heads. 'You're too poor,' they said.

Bert the cook laughed sarcastically.

I took the three best haddocks I could find from the morning's catch and set out for the farm.

They shook their heads after me. The skipper took his pipe from his mouth and spat — he thought I must have gone out of my mind.

I was astonished at my own resolution. Was I not the shy one of the Kestrel, who dodged into the wheelhouse whenever a pretty girl stood on the pier above and asked were there any scallops to spare?

I walked on through the village with my three sklintering haddocks.

For the first time — between the tailor shop and the kirk — I felt a flutter of fear. The farm I was going to — it was said that queer proud cantankerous folk lived on it. What could a shy fisherman say to the likes of them, with their hills of green and yellow and their ancestors going back to the days of King Hakon?

That stern tree had lately burgeoned with Anna.

For the love of Anna I was approaching Muckle Glebe.

Old Check was taking the shutters from the hotel bar as I went past. It was opening time in the village.

I stood in need of a glass of rum to feed my faltering flame.

'Well,' said the old landlord, as he set the rum before me and took my silver, 'they're still at it. Belfast. Viet-Nam. The Jews and the Arabs. And now Iceland.'

Poor old Check, I thought to myself, worrying about troubles he can do nothing to put right. How terrible to be old and your heart as dry as a cork!

'Well,' I said, drinking down the last of the rum, 'but there must be love songs even in places like that.'

He looked at me as if I was mad. One or two villagers came into the bar. I went out.

As I left the last houses of the village the small simple-witted boy called Oik who lives with his mother and three or four illegitimate brothers and sisters in a war-time hut ran after me. The story is that a horse kicked him. If so, that beast set a spark of great innocence adrift on the world.

'O, mister,' he said, 'where are you going?'

I said I was going to Anna of Muckle Glebe. No point in dissimulating with a boy like Oik.

'Are you going to give Anna them fish?' he said. He looked at the haddocks with round pellucid hungry eyes.

I said it was a present for Anna.

'Anna's the nicest lass in Norday,' said Oik. 'But she tells terrible lies.'

This mingled estimate of Anna's character, coming from such an innocent mouth, intrigued me. I stopped in my tracks and looked at the boy.

'Besides,' said Oik, 'they don't need fish up at Muckle Glebe.'

The three haddocks flashed in the sun. 'Maybe two would be enough for a place like that,' I said. I loosened the string and freed a jaw and gave the smallest fish to Oik.

'Now tell me,' I said, 'what kind of lies does Anna tell?'

But he was off. He did not even pause to thank me. His bare legs flickered across the field. The dog leapt out of the hut to meet him, barking. 'O mam,' he shouted, 'look what I got! That man from the Kestrel has give me a fish!'

I went on till I was out of hearing of the sounds of wonderment and barking.

Quite apart from Anna, I was going to Muckle Glebe to get my silver chain back. Anna had taken it from my neck, between kisses, at the dance on Friday night in the community centre. It was the chain my mother gave me on my seventeenth birthday in January. 'Come up to the farm

Thursday morning,' Anna whispered. 'They're all going to the mart in Kirkwall. We'll be alone. You'll get your chain back then. And something to go with it far more precious, precious. You can bring a fish too, if you like.' And she had sealed the bargain with another marvellous kiss.

I knew then that I could marry no other girl in the world but Anna. The very thought of her, all that week, had been enough to set my spirit trembling.

But how could poverty like mine ever fall like a blessing on that proud house?

My feet went on more slowly.

The shop of Mrs Thomasina Skerry — coats, corned beef, spades, cups, coffee, whisky, salt fish, tobacco, sweets, stamps, newpapers, all in one withered drab hut — stood at the crossroads.

I went in for a packet of fags.

'I like a fish,' said Thomasina, eyeing the couple of slaughtered beauties that swung from my forefinger. I laid them on the floor, out of the way of her all-devouring eye.

'It isn't often we see a Selskay man in this part of the island,' she said. 'I like nothing better than a bit of boiled haddock and butter to my tea.'

I was talking — I knew it — to the most talented gossip in Norday. Certain information about a certain farm could be traded for a firm fresh haddock, I hoped. (The Kestrel, I should explain, visits this island only rarely — we come from Selskay, further to the west — about Norday we know only rumours and legends.) But, even from the warped mouth behind the counter the very names "Muckle Glebe" and "Anna" would come like music: whatever she might say about them.

'I have a message,' I said, 'to a big farm a mile further on.'

'Muckle Glebe,' she said. 'Muckle Glebe. The Taings — a proud lot. A cut above the ordinary. O, very hoity-toity — you would think they were gentry, or something. Let me tell you, they have their faults and their failings like everybody else. The great-grandfather of the present Taing was an orra-boy, a dung spreader. O, I could tell you a thing or two. . . . I haven't been keeping well in my health lately — my stomach — "a light diet", Dr Scott says — "fish, for example", he says.'

'Maybe what you say is true,' I said, 'or maybe it isn't, but there's one member of that family that no tongue could ever blacken, and that's Anna Taing'. . . . My lips trembled as I pronounced the blessed name.

Mistress Skerry's eyes widened. 'O, is that so!' she cried. 'Indeed! Anna Taing. I could tell you things about Anna Taing, mister. But I'm saying nothing. It's best to keep silence. In this island the truth isn't welcome. My tongue, it's got me into trouble before now. . . The great thing with fish is that you can use the water you boil it in for soup, and make patties with the left-over bits. The cat, he generally eats the head.'

'What you say,' I said, "will go no further'. . . And I bent down and freed another haddock-jaw from the string and held it up among her sweetie-jars and loaves and fair-isle jerseys.

We admired the beautiful silver-grey shape together for three long seconds.

'Well,' she said. 'I'll tell you. It's general knowledge anyway.'

The fish was hers. She laid it on an old newspaper behind the counter — wiped her hands on her apron — licked her lips — and told me a bad story.

A student from Edinburgh had worked all last summer at Muckle Glebe, from hay-time to harvest. Whenever he got leave to work, that is, for wasn't that little tart of an Anna running after him, from field to byre, and more than running after him once it got dark and the farm work was done. Thomasina had heard it from this customer and that, but she saw the proof of it herself at the Agricultural Show. Hundreds of folk there, going and coming: and there, in the midst of all the people and animals, in the broad light of noon, stood Anna of Muckle Glebe and the student, with their arms tight around one another, and kissing every minute regularly as if to make sure their mouths were still there. Love is for night and the stars. It had been a public disgrace.

But then, Anna Taing was and always had been a man-mad little slut. There was hardly a lad in the island that hadn't been out with her. She would go with any Tom, Dick or Harry. There was that hawker that had been in the island — a right low-looking tyke — wasn't she seen knocking at his caravan door at midnight one night. . .

But she still wrote to this student. She still kept up with him. And the folk up at Muckle Glebe, they were right pleased whenever the typed letters with the Edinburgh post-mark came. 'Because, you see,' said Mrs Thomasina Skerry, 'they're a nest of snobs up at that place, and what a grand catch it would be for their Anna — somebody who's going to be a lawyer or a doctor.'

Her rapturous narrative over, she counselled me, whatever my business was at Muckle Glebe, not to breathe a syllable of what she had said.

My throat worked on this gall for a full minute.

'You're nothing but a damned old scandal-monger,' I shouted. And picked up the sole remaining haddock. And made haste to shake the dust of bananas and wheat and cloves and tea and wool from my feet. And left a patch of slime on her shop floor.

At the door of the farm of Muckle Glebe I set down my gift and knocked. No one answered, but I had the feeling that eyes were watching from curtain edges. I knocked again. (Surely there was no duplicity in the true gentle fun-loving heart that had unfolded itself to me at the dance in the community centre — it was impossible — and the world was full of evil old hags.) I knocked again.

This time the door was opened by a young woman — a sister, obviously, and about six sour years older.

She gave me the coldest of looks.

I asked for Anna.

I felt immediately what impudence it was for a common fisherman to come enquiring about one of the daughters of this ancient farm that had a coat-of-arms carved over the lintel.

'My sister Anna,' she said, 'flew to Kirkwall this morning. From Kirkwall she will be flying to Edinburgh. In Edinburgh, for your information, she is to be engaged to Mr. Andrew Blair, a veterinary student. It will be announced in "The Scotsman".'

I mentioned, trembling, a silver chain. She said she knew nothing about silver chains.

She shut the door in my face. When I turned to go, I discovered that the four cats of Muckle Glebe had reduced the firmest and fattest of my haddocks to a jagged skeleton.

George Mackay Brown

Questions

1. What do you feel the 'three sklintering haddocks' symbolise? What is the significance of the three fish being reduced to one as the fisherman receives information which gradually destroys his confidence in Anna?

2. What is symbolised by the fact that the house of Mrs Thomasina Skerry 'stood at the crossroads'? How might this relate to the feelings and hopes of the fisherman?

3. After the fisherman hears the scandalous stories about Anna, he picks up his fish which 'left a patch of slime on her shop floor'. How might the 'patch of slime' be seen as symbolic?

4. At the end of the story, his fish is 'reduced to a jagged skeleton'. Of what do you think this is a symbol?

5. We are told that it is the 'cats of Muckle Glebe' who have destroyed his last fish. Whom might the cats symbolise?

6. Consider the title of the story, *Silver*. In the story the boy lets Anna take his silver chain, and his three fish are silver in colour. But the title could also be seen as a symbol.

    Here are some connotations of silver:

    - Money
    - Second best
    - Betrayal (In the Bible, Judas betrayed Jesus for thirty pieces of silver.)

    Suggest how each of these might be appropriate to the story.

(3) TITLES

In the section on character, the author's choice of characters' names was looked at. Similarly, the title of a novel may provide a useful starting point for discussion.

In the six novels of Jane Austen, for example, one, *Emma*, is called by the same name as the heroine. Two others, *Mansfield Park* and *Northanger Abbey* are named after major settings of the books. However the other three have titles which refer to themes. *Pride and Prejudice* is an interesting one. The first draft of this novel was entitled *First Impressions*. Austen decided to change it to reflect more precisely the themes of her novel. In addition to summarising the themes, the terms of the title can be seen as referring to the leading characters, with Mr Darcy representing pride and Elizabeth, prejudice. Her two other novels, *Sense and Sensibility* and *Persuasion,* also have titles which reveal themes. Analysing the implications of these titles would be rewarding.

Emily Brontë's famous novel *Wuthering Heights* is named after a house which features in the book. However it also has a symbolic significance. 'Wuthering' means 'stormy', and so the title also implies the emotional storms described in the book.

Charles Dickens chose a similar technique with his novel entitled *Bleak House.* The name refers to a grand house in the book. The inhabitants are wealthy but have guilty secrets which eventually destroy them. The title can also be seen as a metaphor for the world of English law which Dickens attacks in the novel for the misery which it brings to people who become caught up in it.

A good example of a modern novel whose author has chosen a title with thought-provoking implications is *Regeneration* by Pat Barker. The novel is set during the first world war in Craiglockhart Hospital in Edinburgh, where a psychiatrist is treating men suffering from shell-shock. Can you think of various applications of this title?

For Practice

1. In pairs or groups, consider the significance of the titles of the following novels. Some hints are given to help you.

    (a) *All Quiet on the Western Front* by Erich Maria Remarque. (See the outline on pages 65–67.)

    (b) *A Room with a View.* (This novel by E.M. Forster describes a young girl who goes on holiday to Florence in Italy. There she meets new people and has new experiences which widen her horizons. The first reference to 'the room with a view' comes at the start of the novel where the girl's companion complains that their hotel room does not have a view. Another guest offers to exchange his room which does have a view. Can you suggest how the title might also be a metaphor?)

    (c) *The Millstone* by Margaret Drabble. (This novel concerns a teenage girl who has an illegitimate baby.)

    (d) *Sunset Song* by Lewis Grassic Gibbon. (The novel describes a young woman growing up in a farming community before and during the first world war. As a result of the war, the community decays. Her husband is killed. Consider the connotations of 'sunset' and also the idea of a 'swan song'.)

    (e) *Schindler's Ark* by Thomas Keneally. (Look at the outline on pages 87–88.)

2. In pairs or groups, write down all the titles of novels you have recently read. Discuss how helpful the titles might be in writing a review of the book.

PART TWO

ANALYSING
THE
NOVEL

WRITING THE REVIEW

> What should my review deal with? Are there any particular points a marker will look for?

This depends on the type of review that your course requires. As was explained on page 4, there are different types of book review which you may have to write as part of an English course. Read the instructions you are given carefully or consult your teacher or tutor to find out which type is appropriate for you.

Type 1: The general review

The first type is a general analysis and appraisal of a whole book. This will include a brief summary, and consider all the aspects of the book, such as characters, setting, style, and theme.

Type 2: The topic-based review

The second type will ask you to focus on a particular aspect of a text and to examine it in detail, although you will also be expected to show knowledge of the whole text within the context of this discussion.

Type 3: The comparison

The third type of review involves comparing and contrasting two or more texts. Usually this will adopt the same approach as **Type 2**, and focus on a particular aspect of each of your texts, rather than attempt to compare each text in its entirety.

What should *not* be included in a review?

Do not include material which is not directly related to the text. For example, a common error is to start a review with a paragraph about the author's life. Only refer to biographical details if these are directly relevant to your discussion of the text.

Checklist of required elements in a review:

- Knowledge of the text

- A personal response

- Awareness of literary techniques

- Clear, accurate expression in continuous prose

---

(1) KNOWLEDGE OF THE TEXT

Your review must show that you know the whole text: never try to write a review on a text you have not read all the way through. Your lack of knowledge will be found out! You must be prepared to read the whole text carefully, and, in the case of review Types 2 and 3, to reread your text(s), focusing on your special topic. It is strongly advised that you buy your own copy of a review text so that you can annotate it as you read. A good idea is to write a one-sentence outline of each chapter as you complete it. This will make it easy to find episodes or scenes you may wish to refer back to later.

Be accurate! It is important to concentrate on details such as spelling names of characters and places correctly.

You should illustrate your knowledge of the text with direct references and quotations. A 'direct reference' is where you pinpoint a particular scene or episode in support of an argument.

If you were referring to the character of John Reed in an essay on Charlotte Brontë's novel *Jane Eyre*, for example, you might state that he is a repulsive bully whose ill treatment of Jane arouses sympathy and indignation on her behalf. But on its own this would be rather vague and you should support your statements with evidence in the form of direct reference: 'as can be seen in the episode in Chapter 1 where he knocks her down because she has simply been reading a book'.

Using some direct quotation will strengthen your evidence. On the whole it is better to keep your quotations short. Try incorporating a few words into your own sentences rather than simply copying out sentences from the original.

For example, John Reed comes across as a cowardly mother's boy who is always threatening to 'tell Mamma'.

(2) PERSONAL RESPONSE

Your appreciation of the writer's craft will become apparent in the expression of your personal response. You can do this directly with expressions such as 'I enjoyed the way in which the writer . . .'. More economically, you can show your feelings by the use of emotive words such as 'moving', 'touching', 'gripping', 'thought-provoking', 'disturbing' etc. to describe the effect of the book. Your personal response should be woven throughout your review, not simply tacked on at the end.

For Practice

Read the following extract from *Jane Eyre* by Charlotte Brontë, and then answer the questions.

Jane is a ten-year-old orphan who is living at the home of her aunt, Mrs Reed, along with her three Reed cousins, Eliza, Georgiana and John, who is fourteen and big for his age. When the story opens, Jane is hiding from them behind the curtains on a window seat in the breakfast-room, reading a book.

The breakfast-room door opened.

"Boh! Madam Mope!" cried the voice of John Reed; then he paused: he found the room apparently empty.

5 "Where is she?" he continued. "Lizzy! Georgy! (calling to his sisters) Jane is not here. Tell mamma she is run out into the rain — bad animal!"

"It is as well I drew the curtain," thought I; and I wished fervently he might not discover my hiding
10 place. Nor would John Reed have found it out himself; but Eliza just put her head in at the door, and said at once — "She is in the window seat, to be sure, Jack."

And I came out immediately, for I trembled at the
15 idea of being dragged forth by the said Jack.

"What do you want?" I asked, with awkward diffidence.

"Say, 'What do you want, Master Reed?'" was the answer. "I want you to come here;" and seating
20 himself in an armchair, he intimated by a gesture that I was to approach and stand before him.

Lines 1–15 describe stage one of the scene, where Jane dreads being found.

1. (a) What do John's words reveal about him as a character?

   (b) What feelings do John's insults arouse in the reader?

2. (a) What do the words 'wished fervently' (line 9) reveal about Jane's feelings?

   (b) Pick out another expression from lines 1–15 that shows intense feeling in Jane.

Lines 16–48 describe the first part of the encounter between Jane and John.

Habitually obedient to John, I came up to his chair. He spent some three minutes in thrusting out his tongue at me as far as he could without damaging
25 the roots. I knew he would soon strike, and while dreading the blow, I mused on the disgusting and ugly appearance of him who would presently deal it. I wonder if he read that notion in my face; for, all at once, without speaking, he struck suddenly and
30 strongly. I tottered, and stepped back a step or two from his chair.

"That is for your impudence in answering mamma a while since," said he, "and for your sneaking way of getting behind curtains, and for the look you had
35 in your eyes two minutes since, you rat!"

Accustomed to John Reed's abuse, I never had an idea of replying to it; my care was how to endure the blow which would certainly follow the insult.

"What were you doing behind the curtain?" he
40 asked.

"I was reading."

"Show the book."

I returned to the window and fetched it.

"You have no business to take our books: you are
45 a dependant; you have no money; your father left you none; you ought to beg. Now, I'll teach you to rummage my book-shelves. Go and stand by the door, out of the way of the mirror and the windows."

3. (a) 'Habitually obedient to John' (line 22). What does this tell us about the bullying situation?
   (b) What phrase later in this section (lines 16–48) confirms this?
   (c) How do these phrases affect our feelings towards the two characters?

4. (a) List some of the ways in which John humiliates Jane.
   (b) Assess how each of these makes you feel towards John.

5. (a) We admire the calm dignified way in which Jane responds to John's cruelty. List the reactions of Jane which arouse this response in the reader.

Lines 50–74 describe the climax of John's assault on Jane and the way in which she eventually retaliates both verbally and physically.

50 I did so, not at first aware what was his intention; but when I saw him lift and poise the book and stand in act to hurl it, I instinctively started aside with a cry of alarm — not soon enough, however; the volume was flung, it hit me, and I fell, striking
55 my head against the door and cutting it. The cut bled, the pain was sharp: my terror had passed its climax; other feelings succeeded.

'Empathy' is the ability to feel the suffering of another. The author enables us to feel empathy for Jane by describing her physical pain in precise detail.

"Wicked and cruel boy!" I said. "You are like a murderer — you are like a slave-driver — you are
60 like the Roman emperors!"

6. *Pick out the phrases which are effective in enabling us to empathise with Jane.*

"What! What!" he cried. "Did she say that to me? Did you hear her, Eliza and Georgiana? Won't I tell mamma? But first —"

7. *Sum up your feelings for Jane as she finally starts answering him back. (lines 58 – 60)*

He ran headlong at me; I felt him grasp my hair
65 and my shoulder. I really saw in him a tyrant — a murderer. I felt a drop or two of blood from my head trickle down my neck, and was sensible of pungent suffering. These sensations for the time predominated over fear. I don't very well know
70 what I did with my hands, but he called me "Rat! Rat!" and bellowed out loud. Aid was near him; Eliza and Georgiana had run for Mrs Reed; she now came upon the scene, followed by Bessie and her maid. We were parted; I heard the words,

8. *John immediately shouts for help when Jane fights back even though she is much smaller than he is. John's mother and Bessie, the servant, side with him. Explain your own personal response to the last sentence in the passage. ("Dear! dear!" etc.)*

75 "Dear! dear! What a fury to fly at Master John!"

9. *Write a paragraph, describing your response to the whole scene, explaining how the author has aroused different feelings in you towards Jane Eyre and John Reed.*

(3) AWARENESS OF LITERARY TECHNIQUES

Your essay should include discussion of literary techniques and you should be able both to identify these by their technical terms and to comment on the effect of them.

For Practice

The following techniques are all used by Charlotte Brontë in the extract from *Jane Eyre* printed on the previous pages. Can you pick an example and make a brief comment on the effect of each?

- Vivid Characterisation
- Narrative in the first person
- Direct speech / Dialogue
- Climax
- Effective Sentence structure
- Irony

(4) EXPRESSION

Good expression will boost your mark. You must aim to write clearly and fluently, and to vary your style, just as you would aim to do in a piece of creative writing.

- Write in *paragraphs*. Structure and develop these clearly. Begin with a topic sentence, and then develop and expand your ideas.
- Structure your essay logically. Pay attention to *linkage*.
- Write in *formal* style.
- *Avoid slang*, particularly expressions such as 'great', 'brilliant', 'amazing', 'fabulous' or 'fantastic'.

A SPECIMEN PLAN

Type 1: The general review

Below is a plan for a general review which you can adapt to suit the text of your choice. You may spend more time on one area than another if you judge its importance in the book to be worthy of this. You need not include all the sections if you feel any are not relevant to your text. This plan will suit full length works of fiction. If your text is non-fiction or a collection of short stories, look at the advice offered at the end of the plan.

GENERAL REVIEW PLAN

1. **Introduction**

    This should include the title underlined, italicised or enclosed in inverted commas, the author's name and the date the book was written or first published (but not the publisher). Include a few general remarks on the subject matter, genre or theme of the book. It may be relevant to say why you have chosen it. For example, you may have chosen a novel set in a particular part of the country which you are familiar with. Avoid a purely mechanical approach along the lines of 'In this review I will discuss characters, setting, style and theme and I shall present my own opinion in my conclusion.'

2. **Summary**

    In one paragraph say briefly what the book is about. Give a general outline only. Do not attempt to retell the story. Probably the commonest fault in a review is to spend too much time retelling the story. Beware of using the word 'then'.

3. **Structure / Style**

    Mention how the book opens. Explain how the author captures your interest at the very beginning. What plot-lines are begun? Comment on the narrative method the author employs. Is it in first or third person?

    Are any special narrative forms used, such as letters or diary entries? Is there anything noteworthy in the structure such as alternating chapters between first and third person, or between groups of characters? Is the narrative basically 'linear' — in other words, are events told in the order in which they occur — or is there use of flashback? Does the author move back and forth in time? (N.B. Do not mention if any of these things are not used, e.g. 'The author does not use flashback.')

---

4. **Characterisation**

Open with a general sentence about the characters. Describe the main characters in some detail. Give evidence for your comments by mentioning some of the things the characters do or say and how this makes you respond. In particular, consider how the characters change or develop during the story, and what causes these changes. Discuss the relationships between characters and how they develop.

5. **Settings**

Mention the setting in terms of both time and place if these are important to the story. Explain what they contribute to your understanding and enjoyment of the book.

6. **Highlights**

Pick out one or two episodes that you particularly enjoyed and discuss them in some detail. Explain why these sections were memorable to you.

7. **Ending**

Discuss the ending. What happens? Is it predictable or a surprise? Were you pleased or disappointed with the outcome? Was justice done? Were there any loose ends left which made you wonder what would happen next or which might lead on to a sequel?

8. **Conclusion**

Refer to the title of your text again, and sum up your thoughts. Sum up the basic theme or 'message' of the book. Show how the book has provoked you to think about the topic, and if possible suggest some new insights you may have gained from reading the book. Identify the main virtues of the book and what you personally found most interesting or enjoyable. A suitable quotation often makes a stylish and appropriate ending.

Hints on different genres of text:

Non-fiction

If the book you have chosen is non-fiction, you will have to decide which additional features of the book are worth discussing. For example, if you are writing about an autobiography, you would wish to discuss the personality of the author and how it is conveyed by the book. You will also have to approach the section on characterisation differently. The term 'characterisation' is usually applied only to fictional creations. You could, however, discuss the personalities of the people who are described in the book and how they are presented.

Short Story collections

A collection of short stories by a single author can provide rewarding material for a book review. (Collections by different authors are not generally recommended for a book review, unless they follow a common theme.) Try to avoid discussing the stories one by one, but identify common aspects of setting, theme, character, style and so on, giving examples. Some collections may be quite varied, but you should still try to identify points of similarity. It may be useful to contrast stories which illustrate the author's range. Remember that your task is to analyse the stories' appeal to you by explaining their merits in terms of plot, characterisation, setting, style, structure and theme and reveal any insights you may gain from the author's treatment of these.

Type 2: The topic based review

This type of review will require you to choose a particular aspect of a text to discuss in detail. You might choose to focus on characterisation, setting, or theme, for example. It is important that your field of study should be sufficiently narrow that you can investigate it in some depth. At the same time, you should also reveal that you have good knowledge of the text as a whole.

The plan of a **Type 2** review will be determined by your chosen topic, but there are certain basic features which are standard. Your introduction must include the title and the author of the text, and it should also state clearly what your line of argument will be in the review.

Your argument should then proceed logically. It is best to avoid a linear or narrative approach, which may lead to the flaw of 'retelling the story'. Attention to the precise wording of your topic will help avoid this.

Look at these three titles which all focus on the main character in a novel:

(a)   A Study of the development of (character) in the novel (title and author).

(b)   A Study of the factors that cause the character of (character's name) in the novel (title and author) to change and develop.

(c)   A study of the techniques used by (author) to show how the character of (character's name) changes and develops in the novel (title).

If you choose the first title, it may well lead you into the trap of 'retelling the story'. The second and third approaches would both enable you to talk about the novel. However, the third approach will also allow you to show you are aware of the author's craftsmanship. This will make it clear you are not discussing real people, but the author's creations within a work of literature.

Type 3: The comparison

When comparing two or more texts, there are several rules of good practice which you should follow:

Choose compatible texts for your comparison. Firstly, it is advisable to choose texts which are roughly equal in length and / or depth. It is usually less satisfactory to compare, for example, a very long novel with a brief novella, as the richness of the former will tend to overwhelm the shorter text.

Secondly, choose texts which have a clear common feature, so that points of comparison will make a study of the different treatments illuminating. Such texts might be two novels by the same author which show clear contrast in some aspect, or two novels by different authors which have some similarity, such as theme or setting. In **Part 3** of this book there are recommendations of suitable pairings.

As in the case of the **Type 2** review above, careful attention to the wording of your topic will pay dividends. Suitable titles might begin:

A comparative study of the literary techniques / narrative methods used by (authors + texts) to show . . .

A comparative analysis of the presentation of (selected) characters / settings / theme / etc. in (authors + texts).

Give each text equal weight in your comparison. It will be considered a weakness if your discussion lacks balance, and you devote more attention to the analysis of one text than the other.

Synthesise your discussion of the texts. You should deal with your texts simultaneously in an integrated way, rather than discussing first one, then the other (or others) and holding back real comparison till the conclusion.

Plans and drafts

You should retain your plan and drafts of your review as proof of authenticity. Some exam boards require this, and it is always a sensible precaution.

Checklist of good practice:

✓ *Underline the title* of the book whenever you mention it. (Alternatively, enclose it in inverted commas. You may use italics if word-processing.)

✓ Put *quotation marks* around direct quotations.

✓ Be precise! *Support your comments* with direct references and quotations, but keep quotations brief.

✓ Be *positive*! Your task is to show your appreciation and understanding of the merits of a 'tried and tested' text.

✓ Be honest in expressing your *personal response*, but take care a negative response does not reveal an inability to appreciate your text.

✓ Do *not* include any sub-headings in your review. Write in *paragraphs*.

✓ Do *not* include biographical information on the author, unless it relates directly to your argument.

PART THREE

APPRECIATING THE NOVEL

In this section of the book a selection of modern novels will be examined in more detail. All of these are suitable for book reviews and many are appropriate for use as class readers.

Some have been popular in schools for many years, like *Animal Farm*; others were written much more recently, like *Man and Boy*, while several have been made into popular films such as *Breakfast at Tiffany's* which starred Audrey Hepburn, or *The Beach* starring Leonardo di Caprio.

If you are looking for a book to read, the plot outlines should give you an impression of whether a title is likely to appeal to you. If you have to select an aspect of the text to write about, the 'discussion points' will provide possible approaches.

Star ratings

Each book discussed is given a grading of one to five stars according to the level of difficulty of its ideas and its style.

At the most basic level, books marked with a single star are likely to have the following characteristics:

Ideas	Language
One clear and easily identified theme.	Fairly short and simple sentence structures.
A plot which concentrates on events rather than in-depth character analysis.	Straightforward word choice.
	Story is likely to be told in chronological order.
There will tend to be one storyline rather than multiple sub-plots.	

At the other extreme, a book marked with five stars is likely to be considerably more complex:

Ideas	Language
Themes are more complex, and may be implied rather than spelt out explicitly (e.g., through the use of symbolism).	Wider range of vocabulary and sentence structures.
Plot is likely to have various inter-linked strands.	Greater use of subtlety, fewer simplistic techniques.
Emphasis is placed on character development.	A use of a variety of narrative methods rather than one.

All Quiet On The Western Front by Erich Maria Remarque (1929)

The Novel in a Nutshell: Translated from German, the novel tells of the experiences of a young German soldier amid the horrors of trench warfare in World War I. Having joined up at the age of eighteen, Paul Bäumer becomes the last surviving member of his group, only to die just before the armistice in 1918.

Level of difficulty: *Language:* ★★★☆☆   *Ideas:* ★★★☆☆

Number of pages: 192

Summary

The narrator, Paul Bäumer, had joined the army at the age of eighteen along with many of his grammar school classmates after being urged to enlist by their teacher. Paul and his friends, Kropp, Müller and Leer, form a group with four men from working class backgrounds: Tjaden, Westhus, Detering and Katczinsky. At the training camp they are relentlessly bullied by their corporal, Himmelstoss. The night before they leave for duty Paul and his friends beat him up.

When the main action of the novel begins they have been in the army almost two years. They feel sorry for the new recruits whose inexperience causes them to have high casualty rates. The resourceful Katczinsky, who is older than the others, helps Paul's group to survive. The company suffer repeated bombardments, sometimes with gas shells, and are plagued by rats. The French launch a major offensive during which Westhus is fatally wounded.

Shortly afterwards Paul goes on leave. This turns out to be an ordeal. Paul's mother is very ill with cancer, and he feels alienated from those at home who have no idea of the horrors of the front. Following his leave, Paul spends some weeks in a training camp. Nearby there is a camp for Russian prisoners of war who are near to starvation. Paul tries to help them as much as he can.

Paul is relieved to return to his company which is where he feels he now belongs. On patrol in no man's land, Paul takes refuge in a shell hole as he comes under fire. A French soldier joins him and Paul instinctively stabs him with his knife. The man dies slowly and horribly over the next twenty-four hours and Paul is gripped by remorse. Finally Paul gets back to the line. He is shocked at the lack of feeling of the German snipers who pick off men in the enemy lines.

Paul's group are sent to guard a supply dump in a deserted village. They kill some piglets and have a feast, but such rich food after months of poor rations makes them ill. In a bombardment, Kropp and Paul are both hit and they are evacuated to hospital where Kropp's leg is amputated. After another spell of leave, Paul returns to his unit. Casualties escalate during the closing months of the war. Muller and Leer are both killed. Only Paul and Katczinsky out of the original group are left. Then Katczinsky's leg is shattered by a piece of shrapnel. Paul carries him on his back all the way to the dressing station, only to discover Katczinsky is dead, having been hit in the head while he was being carried. Paul himself is killed in October, a month before peace is declared.

Taking a closer look . . .

- *A novel with a message* – All literature teaches us about life, but some novels have a particular moral message to convey. The author intended to write an anti-war novel, exposing the futility, waste and cruelty of the conflict in which he himself had been involved. During Hitler's regime, Remarque's books were burnt as his opinions were unacceptable to the war-mongering Nazis.

- *An effective style* – The book consists of a series of **episodes**, interwoven with **flashbacks**. There are also passages of **reflection**. The novel achieves unity through focusing on the experiences of the narrator, and its structure is shaped by following a vividly portrayed group of characters who are gradually reduced from eight to one.

- The present tense is used throughout, which creates the impression of an 'as-it-happens' commentary on the action. The immediacy of this technique is reinforced by the highly personal tone of the **first person** narrative. On the very last page this changes abruptly and shockingly to the third person, to tell us that Paul, too, has died. There is a moving piece of irony in that the official report of the day of his death was 'All quiet on the Western Front'.

■ It would be interesting to compare this text with one which presents the first world war from the British viewpoint. *Goodbye to All That* by Robert Graves is an autobiography of the poet's own experiences in this war. Another text which offers many similarities is the play *Journey's End* by R.C. Sherrif, which also deals with the end of the war.

Discussion point:

> *How does Remarque effectively convey his anti-war message through the experiences of his narrator? You might consider Paul's development as a character both in terms of his own reflections and his relationships with the other characters.*

Negative number E(Aus)1220 — Chateau Wood Ypres.
Reprinted by kind permission of the Imperial War Museum.

Of Mice and Men by John Steinbeck (1937)

> *The Novel in a Nutshell:* Set in 1930s California, *Of Mice and Men* is the moving story of two ranch workers, George and the simple-minded Lennie, and their dream of owning their own ranch.

> *Level of difficulty:*   Language: ★☆☆☆☆   Ideas: ★☆☆☆☆

> *Number of pages:* 113

Summary

George and Lennie are two workers who travel from ranch to ranch in search of work. Completely dependent on George, the simple-minded Lennie often ends up in trouble as he does not realise his physical strength. They had to leave a place called Weed where Lennie had touched a girl in a red dress, not understanding how this would be misinterpreted. What keeps Lennie happy is George's repetition of the story that one day they will have their own ranch, with cows, pigs and rabbits so that they can feel they belong somewhere, and 'live off the fatta the lan'.

They arrive at the ranch next morning and Lennie is told by George to keep quiet as they might not be hired if the boss discovers that Lennie is not very intelligent. One of the other ranch hands, Curley, takes an instant dislike to Lennie and has, moreover, an attractive but possibly unfaithful wife. George warns Lennie to keep away from her.

Another worker, Slim, has a dog which has given birth to some new pups, and Lennie pleads with George to be allowed one. An old rancher called Candy hears George telling Lennie about their hoped-for ranch, and offers some of his own money to join with them in the project. Curley starts to argue with Slim as Curley suspects him of being with his wife. Lennie is smiling as he is still thinking about the ranch, provoking Curley who suddenly turns on him. Predictably, a fight ensues and Lennie, again underestimating his own strength, crushes Curley's hand.

When the other men go into town on Saturday night, Lennie is left behind and he goes into the barn to talk to Crooks, the Negro stable man, who is also a lonely figure. At first hostile to Lennie, he lets him talk about the dream of a ranch and the rabbits. Old Candy comes in, too, and eventually even Crooks comes round to believing that their dream of a 'little bit of land' could become reality and offers to help them work on their ranch. The three men are then joined by Curley's wife who amuses herself by mocking them in her boredom.

Next day, Lennie is in the barn again, afraid that George will be angry because he has handled one of the puppies too roughly and has killed it. Curley's wife comes in, asking to talk to him as she is lonely. Although George has warned Lennie to keep well away from her, he ends up telling her his dream too. He strokes her hair and, as has happened on previous occasions, panics when she resists. He shakes her so hard that he ends up breaking her neck.

Lennie runs away to a place he and George had agreed on and, when the woman's body is discovered, George goes after him. He is not angry with him, but tells him his favourite story of the ranch once again and shoots him in the back of his head.

Taking a closer look . . .

■ *Dreams and disillusionment* – Steinbeck took the title of the book from the poem *To a Mouse* by Robert Burns:

> *The best-laid schemes o' Mice an' Men,*
> *Gang aft agley.*

This points to the main theme of the book: plans and dreams which do not work out.

> *Discussion points:*
>
> What is George and Lennie's dream?
> Trace how other characters react to it, at first being cynical and then ending up sharing it.
> Was the dream doomed to failure right from the start?

■ *Loneliness* is another theme that runs through the book. Many of the characters in the book — Curley's wife, Crooks, Old Candy — are lonely and isolated, and there is almost a kind of envy of George and Lennie as they are companions for each other. They are also set apart by the fact that they seem to have a purpose in life — they are working towards their own ranch — whereas the others have nothing but a monotonous routine.

> *Discussion point:*
>
> Examine the different forms that loneliness takes in the novel.

■   *The relationship between George and Lennie.*

Lennie is obviously dependent on George. George is dependent on Lennie, too, though in a different way. It is the fact that he travels around with Lennie that gives George a sense of authority, and sets him apart from other itinerant workers. Without Lennie, there is nothing to distinguish George from anyone else: he is destined to become as lonely as Crooks or Candy.

Discussion point:

Examine how George and Lennie are dependent on each other. Why does George end up killing his companion?

Animal Farm by George Orwell (1945)

The Novel in a Nutshell: Animal Farm tells of how animals take over the running of a farm from the human owners. However, the pigs take control and end up exploiting the others even more than the humans did. The story is a fable designed to warn readers how political revolutions rarely achieve their aims.

Level of difficulty: Language: ★☆☆☆☆ Ideas: ★★★☆☆

Number of pages: 120

Summary

Manor Farm is inefficiently run by Mr Jones. One night the oldest pig, Old Major, gathers the animals together and tells them of his dream that a revolution will come about and all animals will be equal. He teaches them a song called 'Beasts of England'. Old Major dies soon after, but the other pigs develop a system of thought called Animalism based on his vision. When the drunken Jones forgets to feed his animals they take over the farm, driving out Jones and his workers. The name is changed to Animal Farm and all animals are enjoined to obey the 'Seven Commandments', the most important one being that 'All animals are equal'.

The pigs are the most intelligent animals and right from the start they take control, inspiring the other animals to take in the harvest in record time. Another success is 'the Battle of the Cowshed', where Jones is defeated in his attempt to repossess his farm.

However, a quarrel develops between two of the leading pigs, Napoleon and Snowball, who has devised an elaborate plan to build a windmill. Snowball is driven away and Napoleon becomes leader, demanding respect and obedience from the other animals. He continues the windmill project but when it collapses blames this on Snowball. Another pig, Squealer, is used as a propagandist to persuade the animals that all is going well. But the pigs move into the farmhouse and ban the singing of 'Beasts of England'. Some of the animals are worried about these developments, but Boxer, the strong cart horse, feels that they must all work as hard as they can.

Gradually the principles of the Revolution are betrayed: the pigs start trading with neighbouring farmers, Frederick and Pilkington; they alter the Commandments and adopt a human lifestyle, drinking alcohol, wearing clothes and eventually walking on two legs. The book ends with the pigs inviting the other farmers to dinner and boasting of how they make their 'workers' work harder and harder for less reward. The farm's name is changed back to Manor Farm. For the other animals, things are just as they were before the Revolution — or even worse, as they no longer have any better future to dream about.

Taking a closer look . . .

- *Animal Farm* has more to say about human beings than animals. It is an **allegory** —that is, a story which can be read on two different levels, with a surface meaning (the story of the animals taking over the farm) and a deeper meaning or message (that revolutions often end up betraying their original ideals).

At the time the book was written, the ideas of the nineteenth century German writer Karl Marx had considerable popularity. Marx elaborated his theories of the social class system and believed that eventually the working classes would take control and run the economy of a country for the equal benefit of all, rather than power and ownership being in the hands of a privileged minority of capitalists. George Orwell had been in Spain during the Civil War of the 1930s and had seen how an attempt to put these aims into practice ended up in chaos, eventually being defeated and replaced by a Fascist government under General Franco.

Before that, there had been a revolution in Russia in 1917 and the monarch (known as the Czar) was replaced by a Bolshevik government based on Marx's theories. However, this regime became increasingly oppressive and cruel under the leadership of Joseph Stalin. In Orwell's story, each of the characters can be seen to represent figures in the history of the Russian Revolution (Old Major = Karl Marx; Snowball = Trotsky; Boxer = the workers, and so on).

In 1844 Karl Marx wrote:

> The worker in his human functions no longer feels himself to be anything but animal. What is animal becomes human and what is human becomes animal.

Orwell may well have had this thought in mind when writing *Animal Farm*.

Discussion point:

What were the ideals of Animalism as summed up in Old Major's speech and the Seven Commandments? Trace how the farm moved further and further away from these ideals.

Discussion point:

Think of other stories in which animals are given human characteristics, such as those told to children like Aesop's fables. Why do you think Orwell chose this method to convey his views about political revolution?

The Old Man and the Sea by Ernest Hemingway (1952)

> *The Novel in a Nutshell:* This short novel tells the story of an old Cuban fisherman's epic struggle to catch a huge fish and bring it back home. It is a tale of heroic struggle against the odds and of a refusal to be defeated.

> Level of difficulty: Language: ★☆☆☆☆   Ideas: ★★☆☆☆

> Number of pages: 109

Summary

Santiago, an impoverished old fisherman, has gone for eighty-four days without catching anything. He is so poor that he lacks even the most basic possessions and relies on a faithful boy who discreetly checks up on him and brings him food. The only pleasures he has are reading the baseball reports in the previous day's paper and reliving the past in his dreams about the lions and Africa. Never one to lose heart, he always believes that success is within his reach if he keeps trying and sets off alone in his skiff (a small boat) in the belief that his 'big fish' must be somewhere.

Alone on the ocean, he sometimes reminisces about the past, such as his success in an arm-wrestling contest with a strongly-built Negro many years ago; sometimes he talks to the birds or imagines the feelings of the fish; at other times he just talks to himself to keep up his spirits.

He hooks a fish which is so large that it tows his boat further out to sea. He displays ingenuity in positioning himself to avoid cramp, and the voyage becomes a test of endurance — who will tire first, the fisherman or the fish? He respects his opponent, calling it 'brother', but is determined to kill it nevertheless. In spite of little food and no sleep, the old man endures until the fish begins to slow and starts circling, an indication that it is dying. He ties it to the side of the skiff but, inevitably, it attracts sharks which he fights off, although not until they have bitten off large chunks of the flesh of the fish.

The old man has won his struggle with the fish, but the irony is that he fails to bring it home intact. When he returns, the other fishermen appreciate what had happened. One measures the carcass and is impressed that it was eighteen feet long. The book ends poignantly, with the boy seeing to the old man's needs and talking with him about the next fishing expedition. The old man falls asleep, dreaming his dreams about the lions. It is, the reader feels, a sleep from which he will not waken.

Taking a closer look . . .

The simplicity of the narrative reminds the reader of a fable and it is certainly true that all kinds of deeper allegorical meanings have been read into it.

■   *Characteristics of the old man* – The first third of the novel concentrates on describing the old man's personality. We learn about his poverty; his optimistic outlook on life in spite of misfortune (he has not caught a fish for 84 days); his dependence on the boy; his previous history; his love of the sea and its creatures.

> *Discussion point:*
>
> In what ways do we feel sorry for the old man and in what ways do we admire him?

- *The themes of struggle and endurance* – Most of the novel deals with the old man's struggle to catch the fish and to bring it home. There is much to admire in his refusal to be defeated and in the ingenuity he shows in coming up with solutions to his problems. The means at his disposal are very limited and he is entirely alone, but he constantly reminds himself to make do with what he has rather than thinking about what he lacks. He is stretched to the limit of his endurance, and then beyond it, to the extent that he can say that it is only because he feels pain that he knows he is alive. Even when the sharks attack his fish and he knows he has lost, his spirit is not crushed. Perhaps the clearest statement of the moral of the story can be found in the old man's comment that a person can be destroyed but not defeated.

> *Discussion point:*
>
> What practical difficulties does the old man face in the course of his fishing trip and how does he try to overcome them?

- *Style and structure* – The book uses simple word choice and sentence structures, as if to reflect the simple outlook on life that the old man has. There are no unnecessary digressions or descriptive passages: Hemingway's prose is reduced to the essentials, just as the old man's existence consists only of the most basic things in life necessary to survival. The structure is simply chronological; there are occasional flashbacks but these too shed light on the themes. For instance, the arm-wrestling episode was an earlier episode in the old man's life where he won through by sheer endurance and refusal to give up.

Did you know . . . ?

Like Santiago in the novel, the author Ernest Hemingway loved fishing. He was also a fan of bullfighting. *The Old Man and the Sea* was first published in a magazine in 1952. Five million copies were sold within 48 hours!

Breakfast at Tiffany's by Truman Capote (1958)

The Novel in a Nutshell: Breakfast at Tiffany's is a short novel (novella) telling the story of a highly unconventional girl called Holly Golightly who lives in a New York apartment and leads a wild lifestyle.

Level of difficulty: *Language:* ★★☆☆☆   *Ideas:* ★★☆☆☆

Number of pages: 100

Summary

An unnamed narrator, now a successful writer, returns to an area of New York where he had lived in an old apartment building some fifteen years previously. The owner of a bar he used to go to tells him that he has heard that his old neighbour, a young woman called Holly Golightly, is now in Africa.

Thereafter, the novel retraces how the narrator came to know Holly. She used to ring his door bell late at night to get access to the building, having forgotten her key. Then one evening, she knocks at his window and comes into his apartment (using the external fire escape characteristic of American 'brownstone' apartment houses). He is initially surprised by her very forward manner. One of the many strange things about Holly is that she receives money from a lawyer for paying regular visits to a man called Sally Tomato who is in prison.

Some time later she invites the narrator to a party in her apartment where he meets O. J. Berman, a Hollywood actors' agent, a striking female companion of Holly's called Mag Wildwood and 'Rusty' Trawler, a wealthy admirer.

Later the narrator meets an older man hanging around the area who turns out to be Doc Golightly, the husband of Holly whose real name was Lulamae Barnes. He describes himself as a horse doctor and says he married her when she was only fourteen but she left him. He almost persuades her to go back to the country with him — but not quite.

Soon after Doc's visit the narrator sees a newspaper report of Rusty Trawler's marriage — though it is to Mag, not Holly. Holly becomes hysterical and throws things round her apartment. The reason, however, turns out not to be because of Rusty's marriage to Mag, but because she has received a telegram that her beloved brother Fred has been killed in the war.

Holly now sets her sights on marrying a rich Brazilian called José but is arrested because of her links with Sally Tomato who controls a world-wide narcotics syndicate. Anonymously, O.J. Berman hires a lawyer to help Holly. Meanwhile, she receives another blow when José writes to say he cannot marry her. Undaunted, she decides to go to Brazil anyway, rather than waste the ticket José had already given her. She hopes to meet another rich admirer there. Unable to persuade her not to go, the narrator goes to the airport with her — in a limousine which Joe Bell, the bar owner, had generously hired for her. En route, Holly releases the stray cat she had rescued, and then regrets it. The narrator promises to search for it and, a long time afterwards, finds it, though by then he has lost touch with Holly. He is left hoping that, like the cat, she has eventually found somewhere she can feel at home.

Taking a closer look . . .

The story traces how the narrator's opinion of Holly changes: initially viewing her as a 'show-off', he comes to view her as both a stranger AND a friend. Nevertheless, she always keeps her sense of mystery.

Holly has many unusual characteristics:

- *Her looks and image:* she always wears dark glasses and is always carefully groomed.
- *Her eccentricities:* she calls the narrator Fred as he reminds her of her brother.
- *Her mysterious past.*
- *Her apparent dishonesty:* O. J. Berman calls her a phony but adds that she is not entirely a phony as she really believes her own stories.
- *Her recklessness:* she steals things from Woolworths for fun.
- *Her rootlessness:* her belongings are in cases and boxes, as if she is ready to move on at any moment. The name Holly (Holiday) Golightly suggests a frivolous approach to life. Before she goes to Brazil, she tells the narrator that she is still searching for somewhere she can call home.
- She suffers from what she calls 'the mean reds', a feeling of depression or angst, which she can only relieve by going to Tiffany's the Jewellers.
- *Her manipulation of people for her own ends:* Berman trains her up for Hollywood but she apparently changes her mind at the last minute. She later claims she was only using Berman for her own purposes.
- *Her attitude to her cat:* Holly rescues a stray cat, which she calls simply 'Cat', and releases him into the back streets before she leaves. This is a **symbolic** episode for she sees the cat as a reflection of herself — independent and belonging nowhere.

Discussion point:

Based on everything we learn about Holly in the course of the story, how far would you agree with O. J. Berman's view that, if she is a 'phony', at least she is a 'genuine' phony?

The Changeling by Robin Jenkins (1958)

The Novel in a Nutshell: A well-meaning school teacher takes a gifted pupil from a severely deprived background on holiday with his family to give him a taste of a better life. However, the boy ends up feeling he belongs nowhere, and in despair, kills himself.

Level of difficulty: Language: ★★★☆☆   Ideas: ★★★☆☆

Number of pages: 189

Summary

Charlie Forbes, a teacher in Glasgow, is impressed with the intelligence of twelve-year-old Tom Curdie whom he knows is being brought up in an appalling slum. Charlie impulsively decides to take Tom on holiday with his own family. The other teachers distrust Tom and try to dissuade Charlie but he is determined. Tom fears kindness which he feels might weaken the tough protective shell he has grown over the years. In order to retain some control he decides to ask two friends to meet up with him during the holiday. To finance his friends' trip, Tom breaks into the school and steals some money which he knows is in Charlie's desk. He is suspected, but coolly denies everything when questioned. Charlie believes Tom is being unjustly accused.

Tom sets off on the holiday with Charlie and his family: his wife, Mary, their children, Gillian and Alistair, and the children's grandmother. At first Charlie is childishly happy and Tom's reserve gradually begins to thaw. However, Mary Forbes resents Tom for taking Charlie's attention away from his own children. Gillian, who is Tom's age, distrusts him as she feels he is manipulating her father.

Tom sings beautifully at a local talent show and wins his heat. However, he then goes into a store. He spends his money on a brooch for Mary, hoping to win her affection, but he also shoplifts two small items. Gillian sees him and tells her parents; however, when she sees the friction it causes between them she pretends she has made it all up. Tom is aware of growing hostility towards him from Charlie as well as Mary. When the final of the talent show arrives, Tom pulls out and goes off to join his friends who have arrived. His unexplained absence angers the Forbes's, and when Gillian admits the shoplifting did happen, they immediately decide to send Tom home.

Tom is now very disturbed. His shoplifting and meeting with his friends had been to remind himself of who he really is, a slum child, but Tom feels he cannot bear to descend to this world again. Too late, Gillian understands and sympathises with Tom's sense of being in limbo. For Tom , the final straw is when his drunken and dirty family arrive unannounced at the Forbes's holiday home, vaguely hoping to blackmail Charlie for what they see as an unnatural interest in Tom. Tom runs off, up the hill. Gillian follows, hoping to comfort him, but Tom, seeing no way out of his dilemma, hangs himself in a shepherd's hut.

Taking a closer look . . .

- *The themes of goodness and innocence destroyed; of good intentions which cause harm.* Charlie's good intentions are flawed: he hopes his kindness to Tom may result in his gaining promotion. However, he does mean well. What leads a kind impulse to have such a tragic outcome? There are several factors that might be considered: Tom's distrust of kindness and his fear of being 'weakened'; Mary Forbes's opposition; Gillian's initial suspicion and jealousy; Tom's family; the discouragement of Charlie's colleagues; the dishonesty and disreputable nature of Tom's friends, Chick and Peerie; Charlie's personality weaknesses; the wide gap between Tom's world and that of the Forbes's; Charlie's mixed motives; Tom's poverty.

> *Discussion point:*
>
> Consider how important these and any other factors are as causes of the tragedy.

■ *Characterisation.* Robin Jenkins creates rounded characters with whom we can sympathise. The three main characters in the book are Tom Curdie, Charlie Forbes and Gillian Forbes. The story is told in the third person, and the author uses an **omniscient** narrative technique which allows us to see into the minds of *all* the characters. For example, in Chapter 13 the **omniscient narrator** explains precisely why Tom had turned to shoplifting.

■ The relationships which develop among the three main characters are complex and interesting. For example, Gillian begins by being Tom's most implacable opponent, but she has much in common with him. Reluctantly, she becomes increasingly drawn to him and is finally the only one who understands him completely. Charlie at first treats Tom as his favourite protégé, but he lacks Gillian's insight. He allows other people's opinions to influence him and ends up completely alienated from Tom.

■ If you enjoyed *The Changeling*, you might also enjoy *The Cone Gatherers* by the same author. It has a similar theme of innocence being destroyed. It tells the tale of a sweet-natured but simple minded hunchback who makes his living collecting cones in the forest, but who is pursued obsessively by an evil game-keeper.

Discussion point:

Trace the development of the relationship of two of the three main characters.

Empire of the Sun by J.G. Ballard (1984)

The Novel in a Nutshell: Empire of the Sun recounts the experiences of a young British boy called Jim in Shanghai during the second World War. It traces how he develops: initially he has a privileged upbringing but his tough experiences in a prison camp make him independent and self-reliant.

Level of difficulty: *Language:* ★★☆☆☆   *Ideas:* ★★★☆☆

Number of pages: 352

Summary

The book begins by describing Jim's comfortable background and his fascination with aircraft. In the initial chapters, he looks forward to the coming war. After the Japanese attack, his parents are taken prisoner and for a time Jim roams around Shanghai, enjoying the freedom to do as he pleases. He meets up with two Americans, Frank and Basie, living on an abandoned ship. They look after him but he becomes aware that they want to exploit him when Basie tries to sell Jim at the market. Jim eventually ends up in a detention centre where he meets up with Basie again. After an arduous journey Jim is transferred to a prison camp.

Part Two of the book covers his experiences at Lunghua camp. Jim meets up with Mr Maxted, whom he had known in pre-war Shanghai. He also meets Dr Ransome who gives him lessons in Latin. Jim works in the kitchen garden and makes himself useful to camp inmates, though this is not always appreciated. In spite of the lack of food he actually enjoys the war and feels a sense of security within the camp. As the war draws to a close, Japanese control of the camp disintegrates. Prisoners are taken back to Shanghai stadium where many die, including Mr Maxted. As at the start of the book, Jim again finds himself wandering on his own, this time in the bombed outskirts of Shanghai where he is able to indulge his love of aircraft by exploring the wrecks of planes. Food drops by the Americans slightly ease the situation. Jim goes back to the nearly deserted camp where he finds some dead prisoners still lying in the prison hospital. Some other prisoners have returned there too, having realised what Jim had known all along, that they actually had greater freedom and security inside the camp than outside it.

Jim returns to Shanghai in a truck laden with US goods which two of the prisoners intend to sell on the black market. However, they are shot by a gang of bandits and Jim is only saved by the fact that he recognises Basie as one of the gang members. A gruesome incident occurs where Jim finds the body of a Japanese pilot and thinks that it has come back to life when he touches it. Eventually, Jim is reunited with his parents and the pre-war lifestyle resumes.

The book ends with Jim about to sail for Britain, a place he had never visited but which he considered 'home'. Yet he knows that part of his mind will always remain in Shanghai.

Taking a closer look . . .

■ *How does Jim's character develop in the course of the book?* Initially a naïve and protected child, he learns how to survive in a wartime situation. It becomes obvious that Jim 'thrived' on change whereas adults found it much harder to adapt. Jim emerges as self-reliant and independent, feeling more at home in ruined battlefields or prison camps than he could ever feel again in his house in Amherst Avenue. On leaving the prison camp he takes with him a few possessions he has collected there but throws them into the water — a symbolic gesture as he had been trying to keep the war alive, and with it the security he had known in the camp.

> *Discussion point:*
>
> Trace the stages of Jim's development towards maturity and identify the most important influences in bringing about this change in his character.

■ *How are other characters affected by the war?* There are, for instance, those who assist other prisoners (Dr. Ransome) while others exploit the situation (Basie).

■ *What has the book to say about the issue of loyalties in wartime?* Jim sees propaganda films but admires the Japanese. Towards the end, he acquires more copies of *Readers' Digest* magazine and updates himself on the war's progress. He remarks that in Europe it was easier to be sure of which side he supported, but loyalties in the war in China were less clear cut.

■ *Is the book autobiography or fiction?* J.G. Ballard has said that he decided not to write *Empire of the Sun* in the first person as he thought he would not have been able to see things from the point of view of a twelve-year old. He also felt his approach would have limited the horizons of the book as everything would have had to be described within the limits of a twelve-year old's understanding. By writing the story as if it is a novel, the reader experiences events as they happen whereas in an autobiography the writer is looking back on the past with hindsight.

> *Discussion point:*
>
> What advantages does the author gain by telling the story from Jim's own viewpoint?

Schindler's Ark by Thomas Keneally (1982)

The Novel in a Nutshell: A German factory owner, Oskar Schindler, saves the lives of over one thousand Polish Jews during the Second World War by setting up his own camp for them, claiming they are essential skilled workers.

Level of difficulty: Language: ★★★☆☆   *Ideas:* ★★★☆☆

Number of pages: 401

Summary

Following the German invasion of Poland in 1939, Oskar Schindler moved to Cracow hoping to make his fortune. The Nazi anti-Jewish policies were coming into effect, with Jews being evicted from their homes and moved into a ghetto (an area reserved for Jews only). Following the advice of a talented Jewish accountant, Itzhak Stern, Schindler took over a small factory which made enamel pots and pans. While Stern  supplied the financial expertise, Schindler's sociable personality and large bribes did the rest. He received contracts to supply the German army, and arranged for unpaid Jewish labour to work in the factory. Schindler lived lavishly on the profits of his enterprise.

Although brutality towards Jews was openly encouraged, Schindler treated his workers respectfully. The German governor of Poland had pledged to destroy the Jewish population, but Schindler promised his staff that with him they would survive.

Schindler's determination to defeat the system became an obsession after he witnessed a brutal massacre in the Cracow ghetto.

The able-bodied Jews from the ghetto, including Schindler's workers, were all moved to a large work camp at Plaszow, ten miles from Cracow with the notorious Amon Goeth as Commandant. Goeth was sadistic and unpredictable and frequently shot prisoners on sight. However, Schindler continued to socialise with him in return for his co-operation. By 1944 the Russian army was advancing. The Plaszow camp was to be closed down and the inmates sent to death-camps such as Auschwitz to be gassed. Schindler arranged to move his machinery back to Brinnlitz, near his home town. At this point the famous 'list' was drawn up of those workers who would move with him. In effect, being on the list would mean survival. Around eleven hundred names were put on the list. These included women and children, who were all alleged to be 'essential skilled workers'. Eventually they arrived at the new factory, although there were terrifying moments when some women were sent to Auschwitz in error. The Jews were still guarded by the S. S. (a branch of the German Army) but they were fed well and treated humanely, so that they all survived until the war ended in 1945.

After the war ended, Schindler's Jewish workers loyally defended him as a 'good German'. Jewish organisations gave him money to start a new business and he was later honoured in Israel as a 'Righteous Person'.

Taking a closer look . . .

■   *The genre of holocaust literature.* The killing of millions of Jews by the Nazis in World War II is known as the 'holocaust'. Many books, both fiction and non-fiction, have been written about this event and form a sub-genre (or minor genre) known as 'holocaust literature'.

Because of their subject matter, these books contain much distressing and disturbing material and *Schindler's Ark* is no exception. The genre has been praised for informing later generations and for celebrating the courage of individuals such as Schindler. Advocates of such books see them as providing a useful warning against such things happening again. Opponents criticise them for keeping old wounds open and promoting ill-feeling among the new generations. Reading about the horrors of the regime can be seen as distasteful.

> *Discussion point:*
>
> How far does *Schindler's Ark* deserve both these positive and negative responses to holocaust literature?

- *The character of Oskar Schindler.* Keneally acknowledges in the book's prologue that he is taking a risk by writing about a virtuous man. Is it true that wicked people are more interesting than good people?

Keneally engages our interest in Oskar in a variety of ways. Firstly, Oskar is presented to us as somebody who ßßis not conventionally 'good'. He is a womaniser, he drinks heavily and is self-indulgent. He resorts to bribery and associates with Nazis. He even joins the Nazi party. Secondly, the technique of suspense is used. Schindler is arrested three times, and he takes many risks. Thirdly, we are intrigued by his struggle with authority, and his ability to get his own way despite the odds.

> *Discussion point:*
>
> To what extent can Oskar Schindler be seen as a modern hero?

- *A style which combines fact and fiction.* Keneally's book is based on fact but includes elements of fiction such as direct speech and details of things such as clothing. Some episodes, such as that of the little girl in the ghetto dressed in red (Chapter 15) seem to be symbolic rather than literally true.

> This style of writing is sometimes knows as 'faction'.

Throughout the book Keneally frequently inserts authorial comments admitting that some of the stories he tells of Schindler may not be true but are part of the mythology that has grown up around Schindler.

Keneally implies that an invented episode may effectively put across the true spirit of a character or event. How far do you agree with this? Do you consider such a technique to be valid, or is it 'cheating'?

Did you know . . .?

Schindler's Ark was filmed in 1993 as *Schindler's List*. The film was directed by Steven Spielberg. It was a massive international success and won 7 Oscars, including the 'Best Film' and 'Best Director' categories.

Cal by Bernard MacLaverty (1983)

> *The Novel in a Nutshell: Cal* is the story of an unemployed nineteen year old Catholic in Belfast who acts as the driver of the getaway car after a Protestant policeman is murdered, yet later finds himself falling in love with the policeman's widow.

Level of difficulty: Language: ★★☆☆☆   *Ideas:* ★★☆☆☆

Number of pages: 154

Summary

Cal McCluskey and his father Shamie, who works in an abattoir, are the only Catholics living on a housing estate in Northern Ireland. Other families have been driven out but Shamie refuses to move. Cal is nineteen years old and is unemployed, ironically having left his job at the abattoir because he hates the sight of blood. To pass the time he goes to the library where he notices a new librarian and overhears her name, Marcella, which he recognises. He begins to visit the library more often on the pretext of borrowing tapes.

Against his will, Cal has been pushed into acting as the driver of a getaway car at robberies carried out by his former school friend, Crilly. He had earlier been the driver when Crilly shot Robert Morton, Marcella's husband, who was a Protestant and a reserve policeman. Meanwhile, a threatening note has been delivered to the McCluskeys telling them to move away from the area.

Cal goes to mass at a different church from his usual one on Sunday and sees Marcella there with her daughter. As her husband had been a Protestant, he had not realised that she might be a Catholic. Later Cal helps his father chop wood to sell round the doors. He goes to the Mortons' farm, hoping to see Marcella but it is her mother-in-law who opens the door. He returns to chop more wood and is offered further labouring work. During this time his home is set on fire but his father is not injured. They go to stay with an elderly relative, but Cal returns to the charred remains to retrieve his father's gun which he hides under the floorboards of a derelict cottage on the Mortons' land. Looking for a place to hide from Crilly, Cal decides to stay in this cottage at night.

His presence is the cottage is eventually discovered, but Marcella and Mrs Morton take pity on him and let him stay, even giving him some of Robert's old clothes. Gradually, Marcella begins to confide in him. The couple have the farm to themselves for a week when Mrs Morton goes away and Cal declares his love to Marcella.

Eventually Crilly catches up with Cal — at the library, where he has planted a bomb inside a book. Later, Crilly and his accomplice Skeffington are arrested; Cal escapes and subsequently tips off the police that there is a bomb in the library. Inevitably, the others implicate Cal in their activities and, after a final evening with Marcella, Cal is arrested on Christmas Eve.

Taking a closer look . . .

■   *The theme of guilt* – Feelings of guilt, fear and unease have been ingrained in Cal for a long time: bullying by Crilly; arguments with his father; hostility in their housing estate. Paradoxically one of the few times he feels safe is when he and Shamie stay overnight at a relative's house after their own home has been set on fire.

The book is centred around one major irony: Cal falls in love with the very woman that he had helped make into a widow.

There is nothing that Cal can do to gain peace of mind. The closer he and Marcella become, the more his guilt intensifies.

Symbolism is used to stress Cal's isolation in the final chapter when he is working on the fences and realises that he is outside the boundary of the farm, 'fencing himself out'.

Cal's desire to pay a price for his actions in the past is so strong that he is actually glad to be arrested at the end of the book, 'paradoxically grateful that at last someone was going to beat him to within an inch of his life'.

Discussion point:

> 'He felt that he had a brand stamped in blood in the middle of his forehead which would take him the rest of his life to purge.' Trace how at each stage of his relationship with Marcella everything that Cal says and does is coloured by his intense feeling of guilt.

Negative number HU 41932 — Soldiers on Riot Control in Northern Ireland.
Reprinted by kind permission of the Imperial War Museum.

The Alchemist by Paulo Coelho (1988)

The Novel in a Nutshell: Paulo Coelho comes from Brazil and *The Alchemist*, first published in English in 1993, has already sold 20 million copies. Coelho, now in his fifties, says he comes from the hippie generation for whom travelling was a way of life, and this is the inspiration behind most of his writing. *The Alchemist* tells of a shepherd boy who travels from Spain through North Africa, in search of a treasure.

Level of difficulty: Language: ★★☆☆☆   Ideas: ★★★☆☆

Number of pages: 177

Summary

Santiago, a shepherd boy in Andalusia, was intended by his parents for the priesthood but he decides that more than anything else he wants to travel and his father, reluctantly, gives him money to buy a flock of sheep. For a time he is happy living out his dream of roaming freely. At Tarifa he meets a beautiful girl and hopes that she will still remember him when he next passes through the town. He also meets an old gypsy woman to whom he relates his recurring dream of a boy telling him to go to the Pyramids of Egypt where he will find a hidden treasure. He agrees to pay her one-tenth of it should he ever find it. Next he meets an old man called Melchizedek who offers to tell him how to find the treasure in return for one-tenth of his flock. He encourages the boy to 'find his destiny' and offers him a black stone, signifying 'yes', and a white stone, signifying 'no', to assist him in reading omens.

Accordingly, he sells his flock and uses the proceeds to sail across to Tangier. However, he is quickly cheated out of his money. He then finds a shop which sells crystal and offers to clean the glasses in the window in return for some food. He ends up staying on and assists the merchant to build up his struggling business. The boy earns enough either to return home and buy a much larger flock of sheep, or to proceed with his journey to the treasure.

A caravan is preparing to leave for Egypt and the boy decides to go. Also in the party is an Englishman with whom he finds much in common, for both believe in omens and both are engaged on a similar search for their destiny — in the Englishman's case, he is seeking an alchemist. The journey through the desert is tiring and dangerous as tribal war is threatened. At length the caravan reaches a secure oasis where the Englishman meets the man he had been seeking, and the boy encounters a girl called Fatima with whom he immediately falls in love. He realises that the war, which seemed a curse, was in fact a blessing as it enabled his path to cross with the woman he was destined to marry. Fatima nevertheless encourages him to continue with his quest first.

The boy sees a vision of an army over-running the oasis, traditionally neutral territory. He tells the oasis chieftains about this and they decide to arm in preparation for an attack. The expected invaders are surrounded and killed and as a reward the boy is given gold and offered a position of honour. But the Alchemist whom the Englishman had visited comes to him and tells him he should sell his camel, buy a horse and set off across the desert on his quest. Once again, the boy is tempted to be content with what he has, to marry Fatima and be a respected figure in the oasis. But the Alchemist reminds him that he will ultimately be unfulfilled if he does not pursue his destiny.

The boy says farewell to Fatima, promising to return to her, and sets off into the desert with the Alchemist to guide him. Just as they appear to be nearing the end of their journey the two are taken for spies and arrested by tribesmen. To buy time, the Alchemist gives them the boy's money and says that in three days' time the boy will be able to transform himself into the wind. There follows a section where the boy converses with the elements and comes to understand the 'Soul of the World'. A huge sandstorm blows up and the boy is transferred to the other side of the camp. His captors, impressed, release him and provide an escort for both the boy and the Alchemist.

Next they stop at a Coptic monastery where the Alchemist uses the kitchen facilities and finally transmutes some lead into gold. The Alchemist and the boy part, and the boy eventually finds the Pyramids. He begins to dig but is attacked by refugees from the tribal wars who steal the piece of gold given to him by the Alchemist. He is given a severe beating which only stops when he tells his attackers why he is there. One of them tells him that he is wasting his time as he himself had had a recurrent dream of finding buried treasure in a ruined church in Spain where shepherds slept with their sheep.

In the Epilogue, the boy therefore returns to the ruined church where he had started; he finds a chest of Spanish gold coins and the book ends with him about to fulfil his promise to give a tenth to the Gypsy woman and to return to claim Fatima.

Taking a closer look . . .

■ *The book as a fable. The Alchemist* clearly draws on the **fable** tradition of story-telling and as such the reader is looking out for a message or moral.

> *Discussion point:*
>
> What are the characteristics of a fable and how does this novel resemble traditional stories of this kind? Does it differ in other ways?

■ *The themes of the book.* While it would be difficult to give a definitive interpretation of all the symbolic episodes in *The Alchemist*, the overall thrust of the book is nevertheless clear. As Paolo Coelho has himself commented, the shepherd boy represents all of us. This, no doubt, is a key reason for the novel's huge popularity: the book deals with themes to which 'Everyman' can relate.

> *Discussion point:*
>
> What has the book to say about questions like whether one's destiny in life is determined in advance; whether events and encounters are significant links in a chain or whether they are merely meaningless coincidences; whether one should stick to the familiar or launch out into the unknown; whether we should be content with things as they are or follow our dreams?

The Remains of the Day by Kazuo Ishiguro (1989)

The Novel in a Nutshell: Written by a writer who was born in Japan but brought up in Britain, the book consists of the reminiscences of a butler who, after 30 years' loyal service, finds it difficult to come to terms with how society has changed and muses on whether he has missed out on other things in life.

Level of difficulty: *Language:* ★★★☆☆ *Ideas:* ★★★☆☆

Number of pages: 245

Summary

The American owner of Darlington Hall, Mr Faraday, intends to make a trip back to the United States and suggests to his butler Stevens that he should borrow the car and go on a motoring holiday during this time. Stevens wishes to do this for two reasons: firstly, he feels that recently he had been failing to meet his own exacting standards as a butler and had made some minor errors in the carrying out of his duties; secondly, he had received a letter from the former housekeeper, Miss Kenton, who had left some years ago and married. He believes this letter hints at her wish to return to Darlington Hall. Stevens tries his best to adapt to the more informal ways of his new employer, but is constantly looking back to the days of Lord Darlington when large scale social gatherings were the norm. Much of the book consists of Stevens' recollections of these days.

His first overnight stop is at a modest guest house in Salisbury where he is taken for someone of status. Here he debates with himself the question of what makes a 'great butler' and, after considering some of the most distinguished past members of his profession, comes to the conclusion that 'dignity' is the key factor, a quality which his own father had embodied to perfection. Stevens believes that this dignity involves the full-time ability to inhabit the profession and to suppress any personal emotions.

This outlook sheds considerable light on his relationship with Miss Kenton, who had left to marry twenty years ago, but was now separated from her husband. Stevens re-reads her letter which nostalgically recalls her days at Darlington Hall. He remembers her arrival in 1922 and how she attempted to befriend him but he remained distant and formal at all times.

A key episode in Stevens' life occurred when a major conference of European delegates was due to be held in the Hall. In the midst of all the preparations, Stevens frequently checked up on Miss Kenton's work, much to her dismay. To add to the difficulties, his ageing father's health was rapidly failing. At an important stage of the proceedings, his father took a stroke and died but Stevens carried on his duties with exceptional dignity. He considers his conduct on that night to be his proudest moment.

Miss Kenton has a very different view, however. Their relationship is strained to the limit over an unpleasant incident where two maids were dismissed because they were Jewish. Miss Kenton had objected strongly and even threatened to resign over the matter. Later, Lord Darlington came to regret his action and, in conversation with Miss Kenton, Stevens admitted that he too had disapproved. She cannot understand why he did not reveal his feelings at the time.

Butler and housekeeper had been in the habit of talking over a cup of cocoa at the end of the day but Stevens never responded to Miss Kenton's attempts to become more friendly with him. At length, Stevens discontinues these evening meetings and Miss Kenton begins to go out of the house in her time off. One night when his Lordship had particularly important guests, including the Prime Minister, she announces to Stevens that she is leaving to get married. As was the case with his father's death, Stevens shows no outward reaction and continues with his duties with his customary dignity. As Stevens' motor trip nears its end, he meets up with Mrs Benn (the former Miss Kenton) only to discover that she has returned to her husband. Although the conversation never becomes too intimate, her references to 'what might have been' lead Stevens to admit to himself — for the first time in his life, perhaps — that his heart was breaking.

The book ends with Stevens unburdening himself to a stranger he meets. He resolves to spend less time looking back and instead to 'practise his bantering skills' so that he can please his new employer.

Taking a closer look . . .

- *Structure of the book.* Set in 1956, the novel is structured around Stevens' motoring trip to the West Country. The book is simply divided into a prologue and six sections according to the places he visits. The events of the journey, however, are not necessarily the most significant parts of the book.

> *Discussion point:*
>
> How much takes place in the present and how much is set in the past?
>
> Is the car journey in effect a metaphor for Stevens' inner journey as he reviews his life and career?

- *The character of Stevens.* Stevens has devoted his life to acting out the role of the poised and dignified butler — not merely when he is in the presence of his employer's guests, but in his private relationships with others, particularly Miss Kenton and even when alone. We rarely see the human being underneath the mask.

The tone, word choice and sentence structures all reflect the precise, pedantic nature of Stevens.

Stevens constantly uses an impersonal tone ('one . . .') and speaks in a restrained and guarded way, never expressing his emotions.

- *The wider social background.* Although Stevens spends so much time analysing his own past actions, on another level his story is representative of the huge social changes that had occurred in Britain in his lifetime. His story is all the more poignant for the fact that he still devotes his existence to living up to a role which no longer has any relevance.

O Caledonia by Elspeth Barker (1991)

> *The Novel in a Nutshell:* Janet is the eldest child of a poor but aristocratic Scottish family. She is tender-hearted and yearns to be loved but she is constantly criticised and misunderstood and seems doomed to be always the outcast. Her life ends melodramatically at the age of sixteen when she is murdered.

Level of difficulty: Language: ★★★☆☆   Ideas: ★★★☆☆

Number of pages: 152

Summary

The book begins with an introductory chapter which presents us with Janet's dead body lying on the stone staircase of the family home. Her murderer is not named at this point, but we are told that he is now in prison for life.

The novel then returns in flashback to Janet's earliest days. Born during the second world war, she is the eldest of five children. Her mother Vera prefers her more feminine daughters, and admits she prefers babies to older children. Janet is clumsy and odd in her ways, and she is compared unfavourably to the others, even by outsiders. This makes Janet jealous and sulky and frequently leads her into naughty behaviour for which she is punished, thus beginning the vicious circle of alienation which will set the pattern for Janet's short life.

After the war her father inherits Auchnasaugh, a huge crumbling castle up north. A condition of his inheritance is that he allows his cousin's wife, Lila, to continue living there. Janet likes Lila, who is also isolated and eccentric: she is Russian and has a weakness for alcohol. Janet's father starts a boys' school which Janet attends but she is teased and feels she is the odd one out.

Janet is then sent to boarding school. She finds it hard to make friends, although eventually she begins to fit in, both by acting as a clown and by helping other girls with their work. She is increasingly troubled by the cruelties of life. She has thoughts of her own death, and even plans her own funeral.

At the age of sixteen Janet leaves school and returns to Auchnasaugh. A little love now comes into Janet's life. She finds a jackdaw chick in the garden and she rears him. She names him 'Claws'. He is rejected by the other birds and Janet can empathise with him for being an outcast. Vera believes she and Janet are now getting on better. She buys Janet clothes and has her hair done but Janet's first ball is not a success. She wears a 'hideous' purple dress, and when a partner makes a pass at her she retreats to read a book.

However, at an inter-school poetry competition she had fallen in love with a boy called Desmond, whose photograph she had obtained from his cousin. This leads to the violent **denouement** of the story. Her father finds the photograph and rips it up when Janet refuses to say who it is. Janet locks herself in her room, and refuses to go on holiday with her family. Left alone, she dresses up in her mother's clothes and starts to drink whisky. She sees a shadowy figure on the stairs and rushes down in the wild hope it might be Desmond. In fact it is Jim, the sinister hunch-backed gardener, who stabs her to death, perhaps mistaking her for Vera or Lila.

Taking a closer look . . .

- *What genre does this book belong to?* Since the opening chapter begins with Janet's murder, and the identity of the murderer is revealed on the last page, we might expect the book to be a 'whodunit'. However, it is really a psychological novel, mainly interested in the complex and lonely character of Janet herself.

- *How does the author present the character of Janet?* Janet is loving and sensitive but she seems unable to arouse love in others, leading to her feeling like an outcast. Ironically, Janet herself is deeply troubled by the cruelty in the world, from the fate of the victims of concentration camps to the frog which she accidentally stabs with the garden fork.

Janet has a difficult relationship with her mother. Although the story is told from Janet's point of view, her mother is almost always referred to as 'Vera', not as 'mother'. What is the significance of this? Is it possible to sympathise with Vera's point of view?

Janet is the eldest of a large family. There are many examples of sibling jealousy and rivalry in the novel, beginning with the episode of the grey donkey in Chapter 1.

■ *How do the style and imagery help in the presentation of the character?* The book has many elements of the 'Gothic' style. There are many settings involving ruins and there are frequent references to death.

There are many images of birds throughout the book and this imagery is closely associated with the character of Janet. For example, there is the description of the dead bird on the family coat of arms and the character of Claws, the pet jackdaw. The birds symbolise aspects of Janet's character such as her vulnerability and her loneliness. At the same time they illustrate other aspects of it, such as her compassion and affectionate nature.

■ A novel which would provide many interesting points of comparison, although written 200 years earlier, is Jane Austen's *Northanger Abbey*. Its heroine, Catherine Morland, is a teenage girl who, like Janet, has an overactive imagination, and who also dreams of love.

Discussion point:

The attitude of the reader to Janet is likely to be very different from the way the characters in the book react to her. Can you describe the difference and account for it?

Paddy Clarke Ha Ha Ha by Roddy Doyle (1993)

> *The Novel in a Nutshell:* This book is a narrative of the childhood experiences of ten year old Paddy Clarke growing up in Ireland in 1968. Entertaining and often humorous in style, the book nevertheless becomes more poignant in its analysis of how young Paddy is affected by the break-up of his parents' marriage.

> *Level of difficulty:* Language: ★★☆☆☆   Ideas: ★★☆☆☆

> *Number of pages:* 282

Outline

The first half of the book brings to life all the typical problems and activities of a ten year old boy. It describes the games played by Paddy and his friends around the housing estate in Barrytown; the mischievous tricks they get up to; the constant questioning and half-understanding of explanations — such as the effect on Paddy's mind of a newspaper headline 'World War Three Looms'; fights with his younger brother Francis, whom he calls Sinbad; fussing about food; pleading with his parents to be allowed a dog and so on.

Much of this is done with humour — such as the episode describing Paddy's dislike of the sandwiches in his packed lunches which he stores in his desk day by day until they grow mouldy.

The book charts how Paddy changes as he grows older. The kind of dares the boys get up to become less innocent; they indulge in shoplifting, generally of items like women's magazines or a packet of Persil which are of no use to them, simply for the thrill and fear the experience induces. Paddy is relieved when they are finally found out and he is punished by his father. Another aspect of his growing up is awareness of the existence of death: a boy from the corporation houses drowns in a pond; Paddy knows of other boys who have lost a parent.

By far the most significant factor in Paddy's development is the deteriorating relationship between his parents, a subject to which the last hundred pages of the book are largely devoted. Arguments have been referred to in passing earlier on, but one morning Paddy notices that the dishes from the previous night are still on the table. The perceptiveness of the child in picking up signals that all is not well between his parents is particularly striking. Eventually his father strikes his mother. Paddy's emotions are confused, as he loves them both.

The gradual breakdown of his parents' marriage hastens Paddy's maturity. He gains a feeling of satisfaction one evening when he defuses a brewing argument. He even stays awake all night listening for a row, causing him to fall asleep in class.

A further consequence is that Paddy looks to his younger brother for emotional reassurance, even to the extent of apologising for kicking him. He finds himself constantly crying. He desperately seeks to be in the company of a particularly tough boy in the school, and revels in the use of coarse language and in smoking. He makes plans to leave home and lists what supplies he would need but this is pre-empted by his father who walks out on the family. He correctly predicts that his mother will now call him the man of the house.

The book ends with a visit from his father before Christmas. He shakes hands with his son — addressing him as Patrick rather than Paddy — and their brief conversation is formal and polite. The title of the book is now made clear: 'Paddy Clarke has no da. Ha ha ha!' is a cruel rhyme used by the other children. The reader now realises that the title refers not to the spontaneous childish happiness of the first half of the book but to the derisive mockery at the end.

Taking a closer look . . .

- *Narrative point of view.* Right from the opening sentence of the book it is clear that Paddy is telling his own story and that he is doing so **retrospectively** — that is, from the point of view of an older person looking back — but as if he is still the age he was when the events took place. Doyle thus limits himself to what could be understood by a child of around ten. This determines much of the word choice and the simple sentence structures. Doyle often succeeds in capturing the speech patterns of a child very effectively.

  > *Discussion point:*
  >
  > Choose some episodes where you are particularly aware of things being seen from the viewpoint of a child. What are the advantages of telling the story in this way?

- *The structure of the book.* There are no chapter divisions and only the occasional gap in the print to mark a break between one section and another. The narrative seems to race ahead, one topic merging into the next with a sometimes confusing rapidity, as if to reflect the way a youngster's mind flits from one subject to another.

  > *Discussion point:*
  >
  > Find out the meaning of the term 'stream of consciousness'. How far does this term apply to the book?

- *The reader's sympathy for Paddy.* The narrative point of view allows us to sympathise with children suffering the trauma of their parents' marital breakdown. While Paddy is quick to sense a tense atmosphere, he is not old enough to understand why this is happening.

  > *Discussion point:*
  >
  > At what points in the book do you feel most sympathy for Paddy? Why?

The Beach by Alex Garland (1996)

> *The Novel in a Nutshell:* Backpackers in Thailand find their way to a hidden beach and set up a community. What begins as an escapist paradise turns into a savage nightmare.

> *Level of difficulty:*   Language: ★★☆☆☆   *Ideas:* ★★★☆☆

> *Number of pages:* 245

Summary

At a backpackers' guesthouse in Bangkok the narrator, Richard, meets a strange Scottish character known as Daffy Duck, who, prior to committing suicide, leaves him a map giving directions to the Beach. Richard tells two other backpackers, a French couple called Etienne and Françoise, and they decide to go there. En route Richard meets two Americans, Sammy and Zeph, who talk to him about the existence of the Beach. A boat is hired but before Richard departs he leaves a copy of the map for Sammy and Zeph. With a few possessions wrapped in bin liners, Richard, Etienne and Françoise swim across to the island where the Beach is rumoured to be. They discover that drugs are being grown there, and that there are guards. They eventually find their way to the beach by jumping from a cliff into a pool beneath, only to discover that they have been observed by a character who introduces himself as Jed. They are taken to the camp where they meet the others. The camp is well-organised, under the leadership of a woman called Sal. The newcomers are soon accepted, symbolised by the presentation of a seashell necklace. The guards, it appears, turn a blind eye to the presence of the community as long as they keep to themselves.

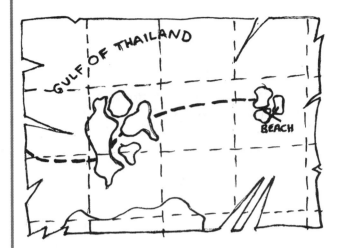

Everything seems idyllic until it is discovered that a boat trip to the mainland for supplies is required (known as the Rice Run). Richard volunteers to go with Jed. This visit makes Richard realise how much he has changed and he is anxious to return to the Beach. However, Jed learns that it is rumoured amongst backpackers that Zeph and Sammy have the map.

Returning to the Beach, Richard's status grows when he kills a shark. Sal discusses her problems with the allocation of work duties with him and asks him to move from fishing to a new duty. This turns out to involve keeping a look-out on the neighbouring island where figures have been spotted, as it is feared that others may attempt to come over. However, Sal is still unaware of Richard's 'indiscretion' with the map.

On returning from a stint of watch duty, Jed and Richard find the camp deserted, with most of their comrades suffering from severe food poisoning. Richard tends to Françoise and kisses her, which Etienne notices.

The atmosphere in the camp is no longer as harmonious as it had been. The problems are compounded when three Swedes, Karl, Sten and Christo, are attacked by a shark when fishing. Christo is missing and Richard goes in search of him, finding him in the underwater passage that connected the beach with the lagoon where the boat was kept. Sten dies and Karl seems to have gone insane while Christo is bleeding internally and is not thought likely to survive.

Sal tells Richard that morale is deteriorating. Richard grows closer to Françoise, and Sal tries desperately to pull the community together. At Sten's funeral Sal delivers a hard-hitting address, three days before the annual 'Tet' festival, celebrated as the birthday of the community.

Meanwhile, Zeph and Sammy, with others, arrive by raft but are killed by the guards. Karl comes out of his coma and runs off but Etienne insists that it is the community's duty to take him to where he can get medical help. Jed, looking after the dying Christo, feels bitter that the others are not interested.

With 'Tet' approaching Sal is anxious for all difficulties to be sorted out and asks Richard to ensure that Karl does not turn up and spoil the party. However, he discovers that Karl has taken the boat and, disillusioned with everything, Richard decides to leave altogether. Etienne and Françoise agree to go with him, and he offers Keaty and Jed — his two best friends on the beach — the chance as well. Richard mixes in large quantities of drugs with the stew being prepared for the meal, planning to cover up his departure. Jed agrees to come, but not if Christo, who is now brain-dead, is still alive. While the others are at the meal Richard slips into the hospital tent and stops Christo breathing.

Just as they are about to leave, the guards burst into the camp; having discovered that Zeph and Sammy had been carrying a map, they angrily assume that the existing community members were encouraging others to come. Then the corpses of the recent arrivals are discovered and, in a drug-induced frenzy Bugs, Sal's boyfriend, and others start to dismember the bodies.

Richard and his friends eventually escape, using the raft brought by Zeph and Sammy's group, and they are picked up by a fishing boat and taken back to Ko Samui. Their respective embassies arrange flights home.

Taking a closer look . . .

The Beach follows in the tradition of books like Lord of the Flies in showing how a perceived paradise can turn out to be anything but perfect. The story charts Richard's growing disillusionment. Richard initially believes that escape through travel works and quickly takes to life on the Beach, wishing that he could stop the world and restart life like this.

Leaving the map for Zeph and Sammy turns out to be Richard's fatal mistake. Relationships deteriorate, and complaints about allocations of duties are as prevalent as in any workplace back home. It proves impossible to keep the Beach completely isolated from the outside world. The savage behaviour at the end of the novel shows that the idyll cannot last and the whole episode has been little more than a drug-fuelled escapist fantasy.

Discussion points:

Examine how the community deteriorates from initial harmony to savagery and disunity.

In interviews the author, Alex Garland, has said that the book is 'anti-traveller' in many ways. He intended *The Beach* to be a criticism of backpacker culture rather than a celebration of it. How far do you agree with this interpretation of the story?

What is the role of Daffy Duck in Richard's development? Are the points in the story where Richard has his imagined conversations with him significant?

Did you know . . . ?

Leonardo di Caprio played Richard in the film version of *The Beach*. He believes that the message of the film is that Richard learns an important lesson: paradise is not some perfect place but is something you can only find within yourself.

Man and Boy by Tony Parsons (1999)

> *The Novel in a Nutshell:* Harry Silver is left to bring up his young son alone when his wife leaves him. Although Harry has always felt less of a man than his father, this experience helps him to attain true maturity.

> *Level of difficulty:* Language: ★★☆☆☆   Ideas: ★★☆☆☆

> *Number of pages:* 344

Summary

The book opens with the birth of Harry Silver's son, Pat. Harry is overjoyed and believes that in becoming a father he is now really a man. However, five years later, as he approaches his thirtieth birthday, Harry seems to be clinging on to his youth. He buys a flashy red sports car and he also has a one-night stand with a young colleague. When his wife Gina finds out about the affair she leaves him at once. Gina accepts a job in Japan, leaving Harry with sole responsibility for Pat. At first Pat misses his mother and has tantrums, but gradually Harry learns to cope and Pat begins to adjust. Shortly afterwards Harry loses his job with a television company, but he accepts this calmly as it enables him to spend more time with Pat.

Harry manages to provide a secure home for Pat and sees him through his first day at school. However, one day when Harry has taken him out to play in a park, Pat falls into an empty swimming pool and suffers concussion. Harry feels enormous guilt, as if he has failed him. Fortunately Pat recovers from his accident and things look up for Harry when he meets a young American woman, Cyd, who is separated from her husband. She turns out to be the mother of Peggy, Pat's best friend at school. Harry also gets another job in television, part-time.

Harry has always had a sense of inferiority when he compares himself to his own father who was a commando in the war and had won a medal for bravery. Although

Harry loves his father very much, he feels he can never match up to him as a 'real' man. Harry's father collapses after chasing some youths who had vandalised Harry's sports car. It turns out he has lung cancer and only a short time to live. At this point Harry's wife Gina returns from Japan with a new partner and wants Pat to come to live with her. Harry refuses. His lawyer assures Harry the courts would grant him custody since Gina had abandoned her son. Harry would like Cyd and Peggy to make up a family with himself and Pat, but Cyd is reluctant to make more changes in Peggy's life.

When Harry's father dies, the grief Harry feels enables him to attain the maturity of real manhood. The final evidence of this is that instead of fighting a court case, he decides voluntarily to give Pat back to Gina. He has learnt to be unselfish and to place Pat's welfare before his own wishes. The book ends on a note of hope with Cyd and Peggy moving in with Harry after Cyd has changed her mind about returning home to America.

Taking a closer look . . .

- *Father / son relationships.* Parsons portrays both the relationship of Harry and Pat and that of Harry and his father very movingly.

- *Manhood and growing up.* The 'man and boy' of the title can refer not only to the two father / son relationships, but also to the two sides of Harry himself. Although Harry recognises certain 'badges' of manhood, such as owning a credit card, possessing a driving licence or becoming a father, he finally realises true maturity is only attained through experiencing and overcoming emotional difficulties. His sacrifice in giving up Pat is just as much an act of heroism as that recognised by his father's war medal.

- *Love.* There are many aspects of love portrayed in the book: romantic / sexual / paternal (love from father to child) / filial (love from child to parent).

- Other novels which focus on parent / child relationships include *Behind the Scenes at the Museum* by Kate Atkinson, *The Wrong Boy* by Willy Russell and *O Caledonia* by Elspeth Barker (discussed on pages 102–103).

Did you know . . . ?

Tony Parsons is a well known journalist and broadcaster. *Man and Boy* topped the best seller list in the year of its publication and has remained in the list ever since.

The Wind Singer by William Nicholson (2000)

> *The Novel in a Nutshell:* Award-winning fantasy adventure in which the Hath twins and a friend embark on a quest to find the 'voice' of a mysterious monument, the 'wind singer' of the title, whose power will bring freedom to their home city of Aramanth.

> *Level of difficulty:* Language: ★☆☆☆☆   Ideas: ★★☆☆☆

> *Number of pages:* 451

Summary

A prologue describes how strangers come to the city of Aramanth and erect a tower. When the wind blows, a small silver device at the top of it 'sings', and the sound spreads delight to all who hear it. The novel then flashes forward in time. The 'wind singer' has long been silent. According to legend, the ferocious army of the Zars had marched against Aramanth and the 'voice' had been surrendered to appease them and their spirit lord, 'the Morah'.

A repressive regime is now in force in Aramanth, which is allegedly under the control of an Emperor, whom no one has ever seen. Every member of society is tested from the age of two, and families are allocated a home in a particular district according to the ratings they achieve, ranging from the white district for the most successful, to the grim grey district for families which are total failures.

On the same day their baby sister, Pinpin, fails her test, the Hath twins, Kestrel and Bowman, forget their homework which causes them to be demoted in their classroom. Kestrel sullenly goes right to the bottom of the class and sits beside Mumpo, a dirty but sweet-natured boy who is ostracised by his class-mates. When her teacher continues to humiliate her, Kestrel rebels completely. In the lunch-break she climbs the tower of the wind singer, and shouts abuse at the regime. She is ordered to report to the Chief Examiner, Maslo Inch. When Kestrel refuses to be intimidated, she is taken down to the Underlake, a vast lake of mud and sewage which forms an underworld below the city. She continues to be defiant and even splashes some of the 'mud' onto the white clothing of Maslo Inch. In a fury he orders that she be taken away. Kestrel discovers she has been condemned to join the 'old children', a group who have been confined so long they have grown old and evil.

Kestrel manages to escape and takes refuge in a tower where she finds a strange old man alone in a room. He tells her he is the Emperor. He is a virtual prisoner, but he gives Kestrel a map, and bids her embark on a quest to the Halls of Morah to retrieve the voice of the wind singer. According to the Emperor, the possession of the voice gives the Morah power over Aramanth, and freedom will be restored when it is returned to the city. Kestrel argues that she is not special in any way, but the Emperor assures her that it is her destiny.

Kestrel makes her way home to find her family being evicted from their house. Wardens are searching for her, but with the help of her twin brother, Bowman, and Mumpo, who has become a devoted follower of Kestrel since she sat beside him in the classroom, Kestrel eludes them and all three set out on the quest.

The children follow a long and hazardous route. Their journey begins in the Underlake, where they must first escape from a group of the old children, who have the ability to sap the strength of anyone they touch. The trio are helped by the friendly Mud People, whose Queen directs them across the plains, and warns them that the Morah must not be awakened or unspeakable evil will be unleashed.

On the plains they are captured by the people of Ombaraka, a vast city on wheels, but are released after they help them defeat their enemy, the Omchaka, another wheeled city. They cross a vast gorge by a crumbling bridge where they are again menaced by the old children, but when the mountain nearby starts erupting, the old children turn and rush into the fire. The twins and Mumpo follow and at last find themselves in the Halls of Morah. There they find the sleeping Morah in the form of an old woman. The voice of the wind singer is a clasp in her hair. Bowman removes it, but one hair is caught, awakening the Morah. The spell is broken. The old children, rejuvenated as the army of the Zars, go on the march intent on killing.

The children must now negotiate the same hazards on their return journey, with the added terror of the robot-like army of the Zars in pursuit. After various further adventures they arrive back in Aramanth and it is Mumpo who replaces the voice of the wind singer. At the magic of its sound, the Zars decay into skeletons and crumble to dust.

Taking a closer look . . .

- *The genre of fantasy.* The novel belongs to the genre known as fantasy which has certain conventions. The setting will be an imaginary, alternative world. The **theme** usually involves a contest of good against evil. The plot will often involve a quest of some kind.

  In *the Wind Singer,* Kestrel says to the Emperor that she is no one special. It is a convention in fantasy novels that the protagonist is 'nobody special'. (Another example is Frodo in Tolkein's *The Lord of the Rings*.) However, the character will have qualities which enable him or her to cope with the challenges which arise. Sometimes these qualities develop or come to the surface as a result of the various trials they must undergo. Kestrel completely changes her attitude to Mumpo, for example.

  > *Discussion point:*
  >
  > Show how the character of Kestrel develops and matures to enable her to achieve the object of her quest.

- *The concept of a 'Utopia'.* A 'utopia' is a country which is seen as an ideal state. Other novels which depict flawed 'utopias' include George Orwell's *Nineteen Eighty-four* and Aldous Huxley's *Brave New World*.

  > *Discussion point:*
  >
  > Consider the ways in which the book reveals the social system of Aramanth is far from ideal. You might examine:
  >
  > - the way the society treats the individual;
  > - the effects of competition on the people of the Grey District;
  > - the way the system brings out the worst in the Haths' neighbours, the Blesh family, and in Dr Batch, the schoolmaster.

Did you know . . . ?

The writer's career has been in television and cinema, and his film scripts include the blockbuster, *Gladiator*.

CHECKLIST OF LITERARY TERMS

allegory — a story that can be understood on two different levels

annotations — notes and explanations written in the margin of a book

climax — build-up to a dramatic or important stage of the story

denouement — a French word meaning the untying of a knot; in a literary context, the word refers to the unravelling of the complexities of a plot, such as the final solution to a mystery

episode — a happening or incident in a narrative, part of a larger sequence of events

fable — usually refers to a story in which animals can talk; there is generally some kind of moral to the story

first person narrative — the story is told from the point of view of one of the characters, using the first person (I)

flashback — a writer departs from his narrative and goes back to something that happened in the past

formal language — a style which uses correct grammar and avoids slang and abbreviations

genre — a branch or category of literature

linear narrative — the events of the story are unfolded to the reader in the order in which they occur

metaphor — a comparison between two different things which are like each other in one or more respects

novel — a full-length fictional narrative portraying characters and actions, often involving more than one story line